Poulton-le-Fylde Lancashire

A Home and a College 1930 - 1983

by Anne Bradley

Contents

		Page
Chapter 1	Poulton and 'the Home' – Harmony and Health	1
Chapter 2	A Resolution becomes a Reality	4
Chapter 3	1963: The Home becomes a College	21
Chapter 4	Continuity of Care	27
Chapter 5	At the Helm: Two ex-Service Academics	39
Chapter 6	Poised for Change	48
Chapter 7	Our Ally – France	54
Chapter 8	Developing Artistic Talents	60
Chapter 9	The Performing Arts	63
Chapter 10	Religious Studies	68
Chapter 11	Coming Out in the Professional World	71
Chapter 12	Living	78
Chapter 13	The Library	82
Chapter 14	Visits, Visitors and Social Style	89
Chapter 15	Spreading	95
Bibliography		103

Acknowledgements

The people who contributed to Mr Heaton their unique memories of the early days are the first to be thanked. They chimed so perfectly with those of the late Thomas Hooley.
Later, tutors and former students took time from busy lives to write their own true stories. It was a pleasure to receive them.
Librarians are natural scavengers and sorters of the past. In the library of the University of Central Lancashire at Preston, all our Poulton collection of news-cuttings and handbills is ordered and cared for by Aidan Turner Bishop who has his neat desk in line with two former Assistant Librarians of Poulton College, Christine Worsley and Ian Sheridan. Their humour and welcoming smiles brighten many a winter day. Thanks to all of them.
Of public libraries, Blackburn was particularly helpful. It was a hand-picked file of news cuttings of local worthies where I easily found references to Joseph Cross.

Thanks also to Anne Smith for putting the script on to disk, and helping to sort out the amalgam of amorphous fact. There was much mercury in the mixture which defied the logical chronology Anne aimed for. As one of the administrators at Poulton said to a lady newly appointed to the library staff: "Congratulations. You will get on very well with Miss Bradley; remember she begins in the middle." I hope you too have got on with this, despite the spider weaving the web from the middle. A.B.

The photographs and illustrations.

There are so many that it would have been good to include, the persons and the background being so attractive, but one had to select.
The Blackpool newspapers have accorded generous use from the archive in the University Library in Preston. Many thanks. Also to individuals we are grateful.
Mr. Hadfields paintings are distributed widely across the world. When he painted these two scenes which his son Mr. Philip Hadfield allows to be used for the front and back covers, his parents lived very near the College in Beech Avenue. A.B.

Introduction

This is the story of a building and a piece of land which proved to be a shrewd investment by trade unionists keen to take care of their workers. It was a co-operative venture with a high aim. Threatened during its birth in the 1920s, it survived economic depression to give back health and enjoyment to workers in the cotton industry. During the Second World War it gave refuge to sick babies and to exhausted Service personnel needing rest and recuperation.

Continuity of the story is provided by the personal memories of people who worked in the complex of buildings behind the trees in Breck Road, Poulton-le-Fylde. As one of the first appointed of the tutorial staff - Librarian - I had written notes about the memories of Thomas Hooley, maintenance engineer of the Home. Mr Robert Heaton, local born, felt the worth of the place and investigated its genealogy, asking for more memories. Mr. Heaton's carefully typed notes from his interviews and his researches into the land bought and the early development of the Home will be added to the catalogued material in the Archives Room at the University Library, Preston. Without his diligence, generosity and a brief note in a church magazine, would the story have been written?

It has a Lancashire flavour with a co-operative spirit throughout. The building came again to the rescue when there was a dearth of teachers in state schools in the 1960s. Later, in the 1970s and 1980s, it took part in the democratic evolution of Higher Education.

Since 1988 it has continued to give service to the community in its reincarnation as the 'home' of Wyre Borough Council – a new borough born in 1974 - which organises full use of it. We thank good fortune, good sense and all who contributed to its survival.

Anne Bradley, Higher Walton
June 2005

Poulton and 'the Home' – Harmony and Health

The friendliest monument to the Lancashire cotton industry, built for human social comfort and rehabilitation after illness, with every advantage of situation, was sited in the late 1920's in what was then a little rural market town in the Fylde four miles from the Irish Sea: Poulton-le-Fylde, anciently a busy port. The power cotton-mills had approached no nearer to it than Kirkham.

There was alarm expressed by some of the residents of the new houses in adjacent Derby Road and certainly by the owner of the large villa next door in Breck Road, that operatives of the mill towns, chiefly women, might not know as visitors to the proposed convalescent home how to behave in a ladylike manner. They might come back to the home on late trains from Blackpool and tell rude stories seated on the upper decks of buses.

Those whose like had - in the hey-day of King Cotton - generated by their unremitting labour a quarter of the exports from these islands did, it is true, occasionally when visiting the Home and feeling better, link arms and dance down the Breck after an evening out. No other scandalous behaviour is reported.

Lancashire has gradually to be persuaded to be overtly proud of its industrial past: one knows of no particular monument dedicated to the memory of thousands of women who brought families up in time spare from using both hands for long hours in the power cotton-mills. There were few people in Lancashire between 1820 and the 1950's who did not have relatives who contributed to this great industry.

If their descendants had been welcomed to a party in 2000 at the Wyre Borough Council Offices - since 1988 occupying the Convalescent Home built for the Amalgamated Weavers - we would need a Millennium Dome to accommodate them all. It is a place that is 'good at parties' and always was from its very beginning, though styles of dancing and music changed. The Convalescent Home services moved out to the Grand Hotel at Morecambe in 1962. In 1963 a Teachers' Training College spread in its walls instead. The Beatles had already galvanised the entertainment world of the young, both in Britain and across the Atlantic.

Chapter 1   Poulton and 'the Home' – Harmony and Health

A summer morning, late 1950's; a large new flag awaits a breeze.
Photo: Blackpool Gazette and Herald

After 20 years, in 1983, another generation of students - recruited for a BA degree rather than BEd (BA courses being latterly Poulton College's main function) - legs still clothed in the enduring fashion of blue cotton, was to move to the Polytechnic in Preston, after prolonged reorganisation of higher education. The college would close; it had always been designated 'temporary.'

During the 'Goodbye to Poulton' party, the Director of the Polytechnic was overheard asking the Principal of the College, Mr Ralph Eaton, "How do you arrange these things?" The party and dance was in full cry in the upstairs room of the building erected near the eighteenth-century house where the Superintendent and Matron of the Home had lived, and where the first Principal of the College (and the College sick-bay) had been accommodated. This hall - the only large room for gatherings apart from the dining-room in the main

2

building - had been skilfully negotiated through planning regulations as a lecture-room, with locker-space beneath. Breck Farm House and its adjacent shippon were demolished in 1969 to make room for this 'New Shippon.' The old shippon had housed too many hilarious entertainments when used as student recreation-space for the name to be easily discarded.

So here the domestic-staff and lecturing-staff blended in merriment unconforming to the researched affinities which the Director, the late Dr Harry Law, had been trained to expect as he cast his eye, directed by his chemistry-trained brain, on the colourful moving scene before him.

Parties grow out of people: the first parties in the convalescent home were part of the therapy. They were held weekly, organised by a Matron gifted in the entertainment arts. But much of their success was due to the established camaraderie of the power cotton-mills and the irrepressible high spirits of the seaside resort of Blackpool, sustained by industrial workers of the North. To people recovering from urban diseases rife in the smoke-laden towns of Burnley and Oldham, how clean and pleasant would seem the bay-windowed rooms of the Home, how sylvan the surroundings. All would conspire to sociability. Later, from 1963 to 1983, a sequence of young adults, most of them from further afield, enjoyed here the most unpolluted air at a Lancashire college and could relax from mental concentration on lawns with rose-laden borders, and in the space foreseen by the Amalgamated Weavers' Association to be a good investment.

Do buildings and places know? Those that were conceived with the best intentions of bringing human health and fuller life, directed and planned by charitable impulses rather than for outward show seem always to ring the right note. You can laugh in them, ideas are born in them: the creative impulse lives on into the future. If shifts of power and fashion, benign neglect or wise care have enabled them to survive, we should cherish them. Happy ghosts live in them.

In the spring and summer of 1963 Miss Mary Wilson - having moved from the University of Keele to assemble, as Principal, the college at Poulton - lived quite alone in the unguarded complex of buildings. She said it was in no sense eerie; the owls were vigilant about their own business in the sycamore trees, and hares scampered at dawn along the tarmac paths of the garden.

A Resolution becomes a Reality

The Background
The land seaward from the gentle rise of the Breck at Poulton is little higher in latitude than Skipool Creek; it was known to locals even in the 1970s to be undrained and boggy. Apart from the LMS railway arriving in 1840 on a dangerous curve from Blackpool (and later, after a major accident, re-routed higher on the Breck) nothing much had happened to disturb its contour since the Romans navigated the Wyre estuary. Cattle could graze on the fields furthest from Breck Farm, whose house faced the roadside, but the land was unsuitable for arable crops.

The Woodlands (formerly Breck Villa)
Neighbour to the farmhouse – which faced the Old Oak public house – but at a secluded distance from it, stood a handsome eighteenth-century house, whose destiny it was to be incorporated into the Amalgamated Weavers' 'Grand Plan' of buildings.

An old postcard view of these buildings on the Breck stimulated Mr Robert Heaton (only ten years old at Sheaf Street School when the Weavers moved to Morecambe in 1962) to begin his researches. They were most meticulous and thorough, and though he has now moved to Cheshire, he continues to make them available for the purposes of this record. We are most grateful to him. It is in the spirit of the place that a Poulton-born man should do so much of the spade-work for the place he loves. He has found out much about the people whose legacy of land and buildings we see today. He found:

Henry Isaacson Parry – born 1841
Though the deeds of the Weavers' property are not complete, they reveal that it was Judge Parry (not to be confused with Judge Edward Abbot Parry who was born nearly 20 years later) who started to bring together the lands the Amalgamated Weavers eventually purchased.

In 1886 Mr Parry had been appointed as Registrar of Lancashire County Court. The importance of the town had been enhanced by this court's being held in Poulton. Mr Parry held the position for 35 years, and was active in the public life of Poulton.

In the summer of 1889 he bought *The Woodlands* - the house which has been incorporated on the north-side of the buildings we now know. During his 28 years living at this house, he bought land to the south and east of it. He also bought two small plots from a Sarah Hyde, where the large villa which became the Education Offices now stands in Breck Road. Lastly, he purchased 26 acres which included Breck Farm. He continued to live at *The Woodlands* until 1919, when he moved to Southport.

The Halliwell family
On the 28th November 1919, Judge Parry sold all his Poulton properties in the Breck area to a mill-owner from Shaw, Oldham for the sum of £8,150. In 1891, Mr Halliwell had married a Miss Jane Dixon of Poulton-le-Fylde at St Chad's church. Mr Halliwell died in 1927, his son Fred then acting as trustee to the estate and also making further acquisitions.

Constructed in 1897 by Judge Parry in front of his house. Known as the Queen Victoria Diamond Jubilee Arch. College minibuses only just scraped through. It was demolished in 1969, together with the farmhouse – to the right of the picture.

Joseph Cross
Joseph Cross was born in 1860. He became, living in Blackburn most of his life, one of those tireless public servants to a great industry which was periodically bedevilled by economic recessions. He died in 1925, revered by all who knew him, both those in the textile and the wider trades union worlds.
He had been secretary for the *Darwen*, and later for the *Blackburn Weavers' Association*s; Vice President of *Blackburn and District Weavers' Association*, and in 1906 was appointed secretary of the *Amalgamated Weavers' Association (AWA)*.
Wider experience came as Labour correspondent to the Board of Trade for the Blackburn district of East Lancashire; he was elected to the committee of the *General Federation of Trades Unions*, and he represented the textile trades unions on the *Advisory Committee for England* under the National Insurance Act. He was a Borough and also a County magistrate.

When in 1906 Joseph Cross was preferred to be secretary of the Northern Council of the *North Counties Weavers' Amalgamation* at the age of 46, two columns of broadsheet of the *Blackburn Weekly Telegraph* read like a eulogy of his career and qualities. So reasonable and persuasive was he, that membership in October 1920 reached a record of 224,000.

"...as the secretary of the *United Factory Workers' Association* he has attended the international congresses held at Ghent, Roubaix, Berlin, Zurich and Milan... he maintains that given new machinery and good twist and yarn, that the staple trade of Lancashire can hold its own with the rest of the world..." *BWT* – March 1906.

His name had been put forward in 1902 when selections were made for parliamentary candidates by the Clitheroe Division Labour Representation committee, but Mr Cross declined and left the field free for David J Shackleton. "...at this moment he might have formed one of the determined band of Labour men at present in the House of Commons..." *BWT* – March 1906.

His range with regard to the effect of national legislation was both wide and specific. In May 1911 the *Blackburn Telegraph* featured his comments about the proposed National Insurance scheme (in his role as representative of the textile unions on the *Advisory Committee for England*) and the Workman's Compensation Act. The annual insurance cost for the engineering firm *Howard and Bullough* at Accrington would be £2,600. "...but it has great social measure...there seemed to be no reason why the contributions and benefits of men and women should not be equal, for both earned the same wages for the same class of work..." He approved the maternity clauses, but he wanted more provision for a girl who might pay into the fund from the age of 15 or 16. She was fully employed and did not require any benefits until she reached the age of 26 or 27 when she gave up her daily occupation on marriage...he saw no reason why an account should not be taken of the benefits she had received.... The state might present her with a suitable wedding gift at a time when it was most needed..." As in all matters, Joseph Cross took the wider view, both economically for employers, and financially and actuarially for all. There was at that time a 'great outcry' that people were delaying marriage.

The special articles about Joseph Cross in local and national newspapers (gathered together in a folder by the Reference Librarian in Blackburn library) all give credit to his great probity of character and practical intelligence. "...His handsome oval face and bright deep-set eyes convey the transparent honesty of purpose that brought all controversial matters to a plain explanation of the points at issue. No man in the whole of the cotton movement was held in higher regard than Cross, and employers invariably spoke of him as a leader always prepared to study carefully the other side of a case in which he happened to be engaged..." *Manchester Guardian* – 13th January 1925.

Joseph Cross had died on the Sunday before that obituary appeared. On the 17th, the *Blackburn Telegraph* reported in detail all the prominent persons of every phase of political, religious, and industrial life gathered at St Joseph's church at Audley for solemn Requiem Mass. "...The mills in the immediate district stopped in order to give the operatives opportunity of witnessing the obsequies of their leader...the streets in the vicinity were thickly lined..." On two-thirds of a column of broadsheet are listed the floral tributes so numerous that they were conveyed in two landaux; "...about one hundred of the representatives walked at the head of the cortège more than a mile, other delegates being accommodated in coaches of which there were between 20 and 30, to the cemetery where there was a large gathering to witness the last rites. Family mourners were numerous (two of his sons had served in the War), so perhaps they all were at the Cooperative Hall afterwards with Sir David Shackleton KCB, and Mr A Henderson MP. The latter spoke for all of his appreciation of the greatness of fidelity and the deep convictions that had characterised one who had been a servant of the people..."

No Blackburn grave monument

The Roman Catholic area of Blackburn cemetery is at the height of the wind-blown ridge. For whatever safety reasons, we do not know, many grave monuments were unofficially removed in the early 1960's. Some undamaged ones were against a wall. Broken stone was placed where the R.C. Chapel used to be. So there is no Blackburn monument to this notable man.

During the 19 years of his secretaryship of the *AWA* (there were 38 weavers' unions based in Lancashire towns) fundraising was begun to provide convalescent facilities after sickness for paid-up members. Efficient management enabled the association to weather the financial storms of the General Strike in 1926. The locked-out miners continued their struggle for six months. The *AWA* made a sum of almost £2,400 in relief-grants to Districts, a grant of £20,000 to the TUC and Miners' Federation funds, and a grant of £5,000 to the Lancashire and Cheshire Miners' Federation. A loan of £30,000 made to the Yorkshire Mineworkers' association was repaid by them in 1927.

The Joseph Cross Memorial Convalescent Home
That a site to build a convalescent home had been secured and an architect appointed by 30th August 1927 was a wonderful achievement of energy and faith in the future of the industry. Sites at Lytham St Annes, Bispham and Blackpool had been inspected, but Poulton was decided upon; the railway station was near at hand to a handsome house surrounded by agricultural land. After the first World War, the latter commodity was cheap and could be regarded as an investment.

The Halliwell Estate: The Woodlands
Mr Frank Halliwell, the Oldham mill-owner, had died in March 1927. It was likely that the union officials who were acting on behalf of the *AWA* knew Mr Halliwell's son, who now managed his father's properties, including one of them - *The Woodlands* - earlier known as *Breck Villa*.

The *Woodlands* Estate, now for sale, comprised almost 4 acres. The house had 6 bedrooms, bathrooms, dining-room, drawing-room, lounge, hall, kitchens, pantries, etc. It would accommodate staff at the proposed home, and was conveyed to the *AWA* at a cost of £5,750.

In September 1929, land from the LMS Railway Company was bought for £850, and in April 1930 there was the final purchase from the Halliwell Estate of 36 acres, which included *Croft House* in Grosvenor Road, and *Breck Farm* for £8,000.

Joseph Cross, who had died in 1925, was not forgotten by the worthy gentlemen of the unions, and the *AWA:* the building that was about to be commissioned was to be named the *Joseph Cross Memorial Convalescent Home.*

The grand design – Architect: J B Thornley of Darwen
Alderman J B Thornley, a senior man, had architectural offices in Darwen, Wigan and Southport. The *Darwen News*, announcing his death with a full account on 2nd November 1932, wrote: "...he had completed designs for mills, factories, day and Sunday schools, churches. Chapels, cooperative stores. Public libraries and amusement halls, as well as palatial residences..." They pointed out two outstanding schemes – the *Joseph Cross Convalescent Home*, and the offices of the *Manchester Unity of Oddfellows*, number 40, Fountain Street, Manchester.

Thornley's buildings, other than the 'palatial residences' (perhaps these survive at Southport?) have not only underpinned early twentieth-century Lancashire culture, but must still give a local character to Lancashire townscapes.

For this prime site in Poulton, edging the lower peaty land to the west, the artist's impression of the architect's vision shows flair and confidence. The design is in the style of the time – mock-Tudor – following the William Morris and Lutyens picturesque tradition. Apart from the unbuilt south residential wing which would have formed a parallel with the one completing the frontage, and which would have enclosed the "ladies' lawn," everything took shape as depicted in the drawing. Thornley had gained the consensus of a powerful committee, far more difficult than meeting the tastes and requests of an individual client. Here was a Darwen man, a professional to be trusted. Flamboyance was there none, but just sufficient variety, curved or straight in the wood-on-plaster of the exterior, to avoid monotony; just enough difference in the pattern of the frieze and in the design of the rosemary-tiled roofs to avoid repetition, but to convey sympathy. The chimneys did not flaunt oversail heads, they had simple recessed courses.

That Thornley was committed to the work is shown in his being willing to share responsibility with the *AWA* for the completion of the building-work when the first builder went bankrupt.

Messrs James Byrom Ltd, of Bury, after various alternative plans had been considered and 27 contractors had submitted tenders, started building in September 1928. It was a firm involved in many large projects, and at one time employed over 1,000 men. At Poulton, they submitted for £61,000. The founder of the firm had died in April 1927. In just over a year on the job, when £25,000 worth of work had been completed, business failure was unavoidable.

Disaster was avoided by the architect and the *AWA* head office dealing with numerous sub-contracts, and employing direct labour. A report in *Blackpool Gazette and Herald* in November 1930 mentions three local builders and suppliers:- Mr William Jackson of Layton for slating and roof-tiling;
         Crossleys of Bispham for handrails and oak stairs;
Messrs Walmsley and Oldham of Fleetwood for painting.

Chapter 2 A Resolution becomes a Reality

The grand design, Architect J.B. Thornley.

A Resolution becomes a Reality Chapter 2

THE AMALGAMATED WEAVERS' ASSOCIATION
THE "JOSEPH CROSS" MEMORIAL
CONVALESCENT HOME.
POULTON-LE-FYLDE.
JOHN B. THORNLEY, ARCHITECT, DARWEN. 1922.

His vision shows flair and confidence.

Chapter 2   A Resolution becomes a Reality

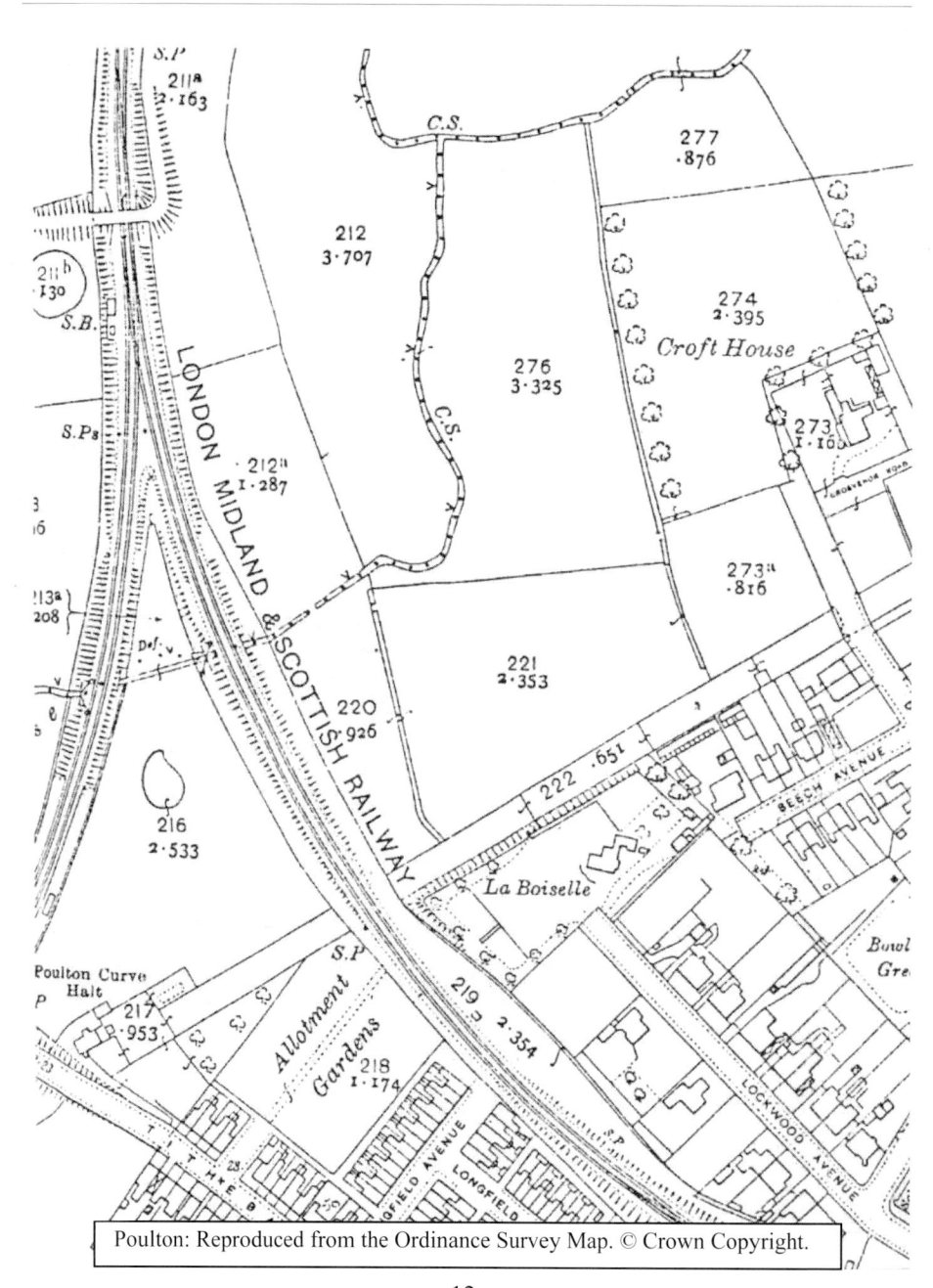

Poulton: Reproduced from the Ordinance Survey Map. © Crown Copyright.

A Resolution becomes a Reality									Chapter 2

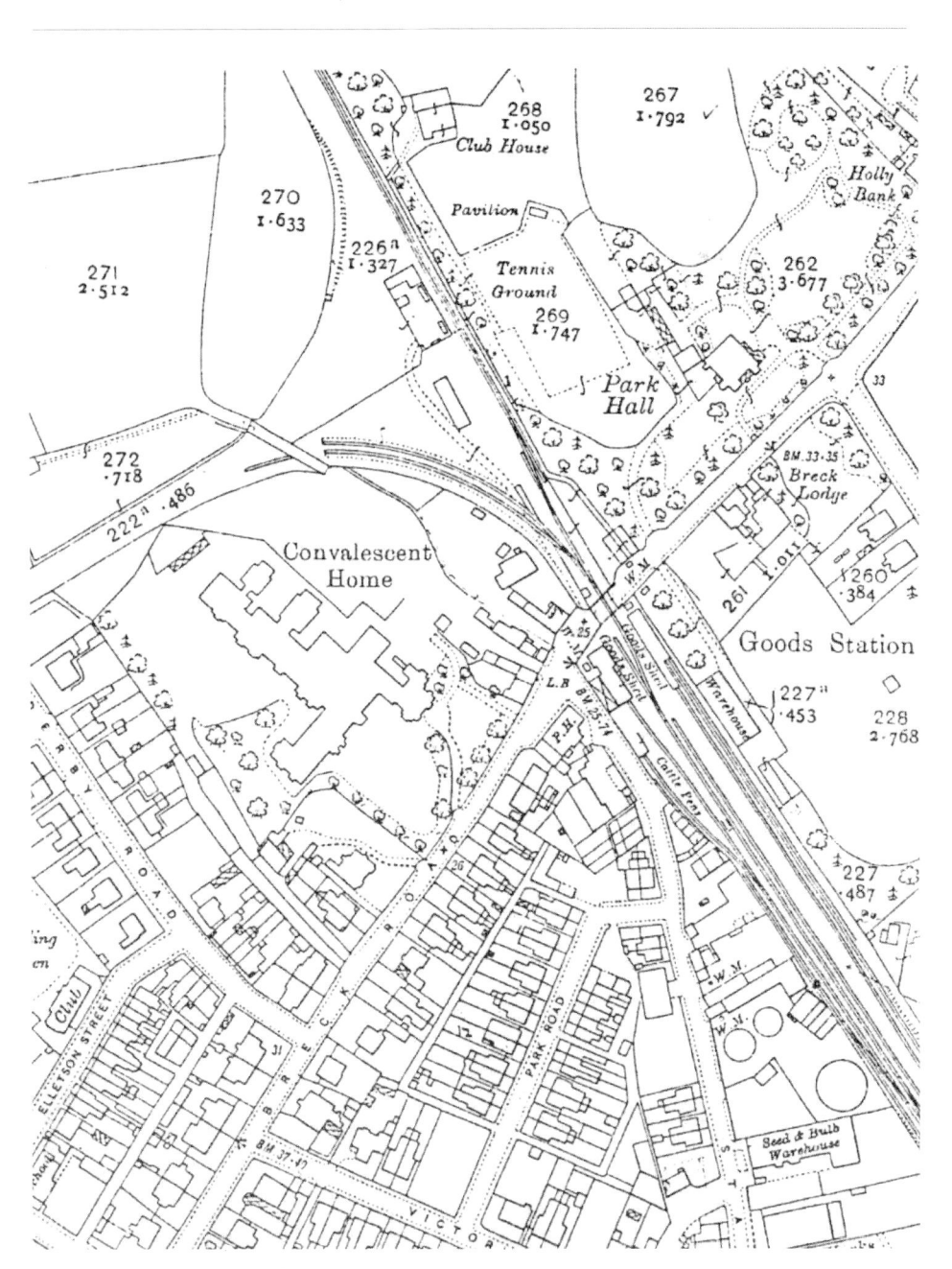

Chapter 2　　　　　　　　　　　　　　　　　　A Resolution becomes a Reality

The building is finished, 1929. Joseph Cross Memorial Convalescent home. The luxurious flower beds are yet to be spread across the front lawn.

A Resolution becomes a Reality   Chapter 2

By April 1930 the *AWA* was confident enough to acquire the remaining 36 acres of the Halliwell Estate. A special order was placed with the *Cooperative Wholesale Society* at Manchester for furniture and fittings costing £7,000. Total costs for building and equipment up to 31st March 1930 were £106,667:8s:6d.

The Amalgamated Weavers Association took careful photos - 1930

The Billiard Room

The Men's Reading Room

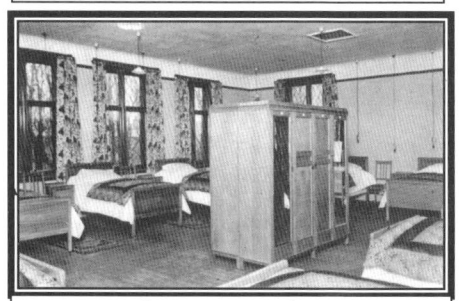

The Men's Dormitory

The Kitchen

The Servery

The Dining Hall

Sir Andrew Naesmith

The Home was well-served by Andrew Naesmith, later Sir Andrew, who rose from mill 'half-timer' to director of the *Iron and Steel Board* and the *Cotton Board*. For 26 years, after the death of Joseph Cross, he was secretary for the *Weavers' Amalgamation*. He saw the Poulton building through to completion and made regular visits, sometimes staying for the weekend. In winter he wore striped trousers and a black jacket, in summer, a light grey suit. Andrew Naesmith lived in a modest council-house in Accrington. The driver of the Wolseley car sent to fetch him felt very let-down by the lack of style of these premises, and was presumably pleased when Sir Andrew moved to a house befitting the dignity of the car and his Union office.

Staffing

Dr A R Murray was appointed Honorary Medical Officer in March 1931. He served over 10 years to be succeeded by Dr F Hall, who served during the latter war years in the 1940s as County Medical Officer of Health when the Convalescent home building was requisitioned.

When the first patient-visitors arrived in March 1931, there had been 1,100 applications for domestic-staff posts. 30 staff were appointed to serve the 250 patients. The number first envisaged had been only 120 patients.

Superintendent: James E. Bury 1931-8; & Matron, Dorcas Ellen Bury 1931-8

Some time before the first patient-visitors arrived, Mr and Mrs Bury began their jobs as Superintendent and Matron, living in the eighteenth-century house – *The Woodlands* – now incorporated into the new building, and used as the administration block. Each had an office. There was also a secretary's room, a doctor's room, a waiting-room and a staff-room. The Boardroom adjoining the house was furnished with solid oak chairs surrounding a large rectangular table with the Chairman's armchair at its head. A door outlet to the drive was from a small adjoining room.

Mr and Mrs Bury were an efficient pair. James Bury was a Bolton man, and his wife originated from Winchester. Mr Bury had been gassed in 1915 during the First World War, and had been discharged from the 10th Scottish Rifles. The diligent researches of Mr Robert Heaton reveal that after experience at various workhouses, until 1918 in the case of Mr Bury, the couple held positions at Swansea at the Tower Lodge Institution (a workhouse infirmary until 1929), and at the Langland Bay Home – from 1922 a convalescent home for miners. They came to Poulton from London, where they supervised a home for goldsmiths and silversmiths. Mr Bury became involved in Poulton public life, and joined one of Poulton's Masonic Lodges. In 1935 he won the North Ward Council election, holding the position as councillor until his death at the early age of 48 on 8th March 1938.

A good team, the Bury couple were used to exercising beneficent power, and strict control of human and material resources. During the seven years of their joint administration, Mrs Bury had been identified as capable of full responsibility, so after her husband's death she was appointed as Matron-in-Charge.

Was it after this, to fill the emotional space of her widowhood, that Dorcas Ellen Bury crammed her office with copper and brass ornaments of every shape and size? Staff to clean them was now completely under her direction. She loved brightness, she loved show. In every way, Matron could spread: her talents in arranging weekly entertainments and concert-nights were generously applied to the job. She arranged fancy-dress parties and dances in the airy refectory. As Mr Heaton's local contributors report: "...one concert-night in the 1950s a few ladies were painted with tan, wearing grass-skirts. Matron sat at the piano with two brass-cymbals attached to her knees. A set of drums was by her side, and also a penny-whistle to hand. A large rope was laid across the stage. Matron started to play her instruments, and all the residents had to join in singing 'Hi-ho, heave-ho!' The ladies in the grass-skirts pulled the rope, no-one knowing what was on the

Mrs. Dorcas Bury was appointed Matron-in-charge of the Home after Superintendent Mr. Bury's death in 1938. She retired in 1960 end. Suddenly there was laughter – a child's toy yacht appeared, tied to the end of the rope…"

Her strict discipline was of a practical kind; to signify that you did not require lunch, you turned your dining-chair round. One morning in the 1950s, a group of ladies was waylaid and did not manage to return in time for lunch. Discipline involved no lunch, and no tea either! Matron ran the Home in the manner of a good Sergeant-Major. If she said, "Tow the line," you did as you were told.

A Mayoral greeting from the residents, Mr. Carey to the right.

In 1940, a Mr Arthur Cyril Carey joined the staff, and assisted generally through the war years. He had come from Rye, Sussex. In 1948 he was appointed as Superintendent of the Home with responsibilities as Secretary, relieving Matron of some duties. She retired to Rossall Road, Cleveleys in February 1960. She died, aged 69, in April 1961.

Administrative style
Reports from former residents convey a consistent impression of freedom and relaxation. The main rooms had been planned with separate recreation-spaces for men and women. The beautiful tree-bordered south lawn was known as the 'Lady Lawn' and the ladies' sitting-room, with its two bay-windows and windowed side-door emerging from it, looked out over the lawn - to which steps descended from two sides.

At mealtimes in the refectory, lit by its eight leaded-light domed roof, men and women sat at separate tables – men on one side, ladies at the other – Matron being in attendance at all times. Seating was companiable, with tables of six persons. After breakfast, there was complete freedom of movement for walks and looking at the village shops. An afternoon trip to Blackpool cost little, even when a pier-show was added, or an afternoon dance in the Tower Ballroom. Men and women did meet on walks, or at the *Royal Oak* public house just across the road. Men from the miners' home in Blackpool would sometimes be there. Always it was a regime of back in the Home at 10 o'clock, and lights out by 10.30pm.

The gardens, with their strong, comfortable seats, some in sheltered bays, would fulfil the needs of those in early recovery from serious illnesses.

Matron Bury had carried the Home through the war years from 3rd September 1939 to de-requisition date – 29th September 1945. On 11th September 1939, Matron had been notified by the County Medical Officer of Health – Dr F Hall – that from 19th September Lancashire County Council would administer the Home as an emergency hospital.

The *AWA* was generous to the war effort. After the Association had paid insurance and rates out of the £1,250 per annum received from the Ministry, net income to the Home was no more than £750 per annum.

The cost of a recuperative holiday

In earlier peace-time, the association had negotiated with the Ministry of Health about pricing. It was agreed to admit to the Home, members of the textile workers' unions (other than the Weavers') on payment of a maintenance charge of 35 shillings (£1.75) per week and the patients paying their own rail-fares.

Members of the *AWA* had a fixed charge of 30 shillings (£1.50) per week, out of which sum the *AWA* paid the rail-fares. Up to April 1937, patients contributed 10 shillings (£0.50) per week towards this charge, the remaining being borne by the special levy-fund (via the district associations) of one penny per member per month.*

Two days after the Ministry of Health surrendered the building officially, patients were again admitted on 1st October 1945. Costs had risen enormously, so a member-patient charge was 35 shillings (£1.75) per week, fares being paid by the patient. For members of other textile unions the charge was 42 shillings (£2.10) per week.

Furthermore, there were fewer applicants. The war economy had offered women a variety of employment; newly-installed machinery in the textile mills needed fewer operatives. Over the years 1931 to 1948, patients recuperating in full care for an average of 2 weeks numbered 14,385. To keep care going until the 1950s, financial aid from the General Fund was needed.

*Edwin Hopwood – *A history of the Lancashire cotton industry and the Amalgamated Weavers Association* – <u>*The Lancashire Weavers' Story*</u> *(1969)*

Chapter 2 — A Resolution becomes a Reality

The renaming of the Home: The Cotton Industry Convalescent Home
In the late 1920s, discussions between the *AWA* and the *Legislative Council of the United Textile Workers' Association* resulted, in 1932, in a financial scheme of no mean proportions: £70,000 was to be paid to the *AWA*, £30,000 put in reserve for a future extension of the Home, and £100,000 to be invested for a maintenance fund.

At the outbreak of war, no agreement had yet been reached. Seven years later, in 1946, progress was made via the solicitors acting for the *Trustees of the Cotton Trade War Memorial Fund*. They pressed for a larger scheme through government departments. The *Cotton Industry War Memorial Act* became law on 21st May 1947. It authorised the formation of a non-profit company to run the Home at Poulton under the name of the *Cotton Industry Convalescent Home*. The *War Memorial Fund* agreed a purchase price of £70,000 to be paid to *AWA*. For a further 15 years long-serving staff at the Home cared for patients under financial direction of the Fund. Until the mid-1950s they coped with restrictions of food and fuel imposed during the war.

Smaller premises less costly to run were sought. At the more northerly seaside resort of Morecambe, the Grand Hotel had been closed in October 1962, and was for sale. It had 44 rooms, 7 with private bathrooms, and the dining-room could accommodate 100 persons. By November of that year, with Mr and Mrs Myers as Superintendent and Matron, the transfer of the Home to Morecambe began.

In the forthcoming winter and early spring, in the complex of buildings behind the trees in Breck road, water ceased to gush into the capacious iron baths and the laundry-boiler, and the heating-systems were quiet. Apart from a few members of staff in turn 'sleeping-in' for security, the wild-life in the gardens ranged alone.

1963: The Home becomes a College

One sunny Saturday afternoon in June 1965, Mr Percy Lord (later Sir Percy Lord) – Director of Education for Lancashire County Council – stood on the tarmac between welcoming lawns and flower-borders. It was the first Open Day of a college to train teachers in primary education. Two years before, he had had to find £126,000 for the building and contents unneeded by the former Home. He was heard to observe approvingly: "The best thing I ever did!" Adult now, the 'war babies' that surrounded him, consumers of concentrated orange-juice and cod-liver oil thanks to the gallant Merchant Navy, unconsciously added their fresh young beauty to the animated scene. To see sensible, responsible professionals-in-training, eager to display their exhibitions mounted in the gracious rooms, seemed to him a fulfilment of his life's work. This building had come to the rescue when there was a dearth of teachers in state schools in the 1960s. Later, in the 1970s and 1980s, it took part in the democratic evolution of Higher Education.

Open Day 25th June 1965. Mr. Peter Long, Senior History Tutor is amused that an historic pipe claims the attention of Professor Stephen Wiseman, Director of School of Education, Manchester University.
Photo: Blackpool Gazette & Herald

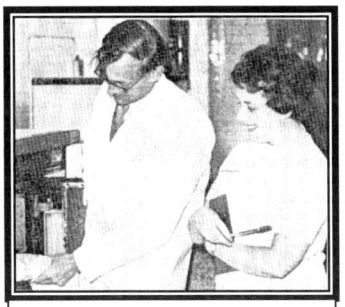

The catering officer, Mr. V. Darwen is watched at work by Miss V. Bennett, the domestic bursar. West Lancs Evening Gazette. 9th. Jan. 1963

The atmosphere on that summer day in 1965 was full of promise. How different from the faces, pale on arrival, of over 14,000 textile-workers, of weary members of the Armed Services put down from the train here at Poulton after the long journey north from the evacuation of Dunkirk in 1940, and persons of various ages to be nursed through infectious diseases.

Although this newly-established college was designated as 'temporary,' perhaps as Prime Minister Mr Harold Macmillan had pronounced, we 'had never had it so good.' After the war ended, 'emergency colleges' had been set up where mature students with much experience of the world had crammed academic and practical work into 4 terms of study.

The output from these, often housed in sheds formerly accommodating Services personnel, had greatly assisted the filling of teacher-vacancies. But it was not sufficient to cope with the increased demands of the 1944 Education Act and the competition of alternative careers offered by the expanding bureaucracies. Men avoided or left an underpaid teaching profession. This was a time when men were still expected to assume sole financial responsibility for their families. They must be attracted back.

1969 The farm buildings and shippon demolished in 1969 to make way for new communal accommadtion known as The New Shippon

Notional uses for the Poulton building had at first been to accommodate residential courses for in-service teachers, then for a women's college offering training in primary education. Before interviewing began however, official attitudes had changed: men must be included as they were less likely to leave their posts for family-care. So men formed one-third of the first year's intake.

The Home and the town welcome the College
How did this hospitable building, secluded from industrial and transport noise, yet only isolated from retail and residential development by its own grounds, cope with the influx of late adolescents, all in perfect health, most of them high-spirited and physically exuberant? It had been planned for, and succeeded in giving, an air of welcome and comfort. On land sloping away to the western view where the sun set beyond Fleetwood, all the main rooms had been designed to catch the light, yet to be protected from glare.
An inviting open-staircase turned off to the left from the entrance-hall, and the long spine-corridor ahead had the luxury (halfway along) of a high window over

1963: The Home becomes a College   Chapter 3

a mansion staircase, dropping graciously down to another well-windowed recess with a revolving-door to the garden.

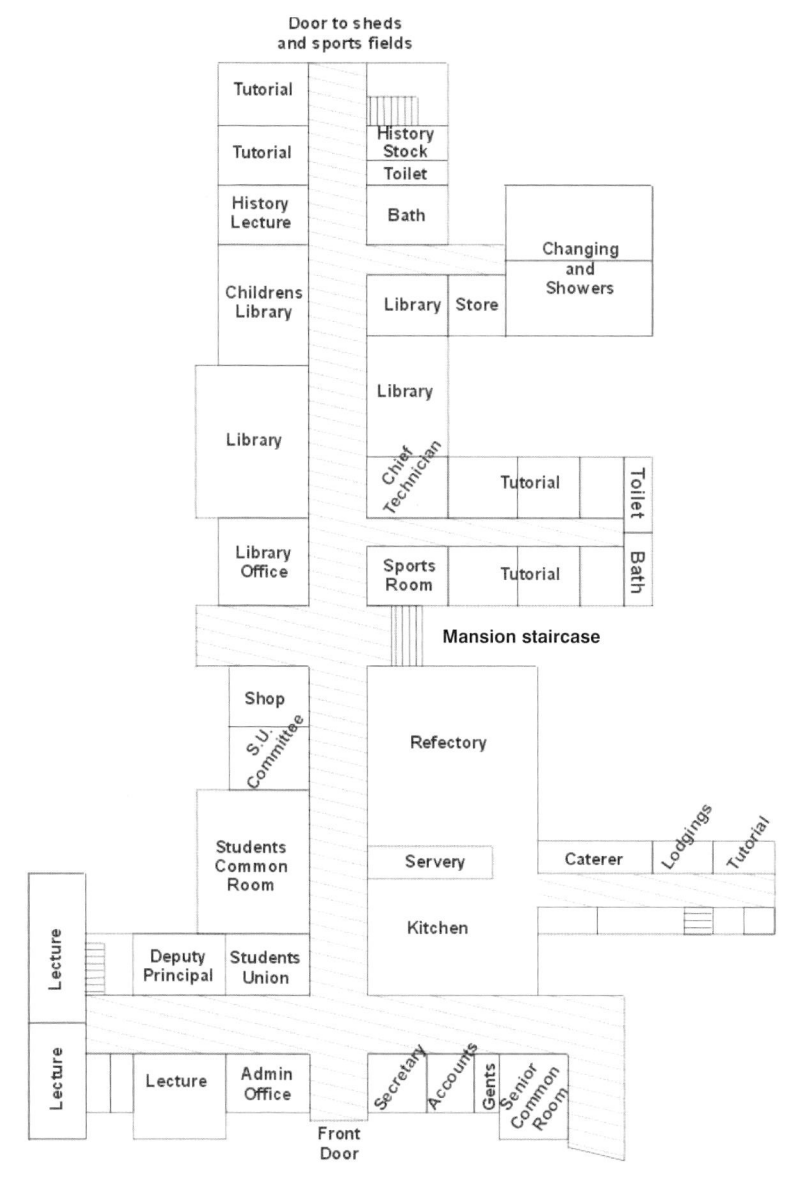

Floor plan showing rooms arranged around the Mansion staircase:

- **Top area (Door to sheds and sports fields):** Tutorial, Tutorial, History Lecture, Childrens Library, Library, Library Office; History Stock, Toilet, Bath, Library, Store, Library, Chief Technician, Sports Room, Tutorial, Tutorial; Changing and Showers, Toilet, Bath
- **Middle:** Mansion staircase
- **Lower area (Front Door):** Shop, S.U. Committee, Students Common Room, Lecture, Deputy Principal, Students Union, Lecture, Lecture, Admin Office; Refectory, Servery, Kitchen, Secretary, Accounts, Gents; Caterer, Lodgings, Tutorial, Senior Common Room

23

Chapter 3   1963: The Home becomes a College

The stained-glass of the staircase light had been removed and transferred to Morecambe, it was said. It was a memorial-window bearing a portrait of Joseph Cross flanked by representative illustrations of the loom, and of the weaving, winding and warping crafts of the cotton industry. The present whereabouts of this tribute are unknown, as the Grand Hotel at Morecambe was demolished. There was another more work-a-day staircase at the 'Fleetwood end' above the door leading to the cellar.

The windowed corridors on both floors, gave, in their 8 foot width, opportunities for meeting and chatting without obstructing passers-by. When the new building - now named the Community Centre - was added after Breck Farm was demolished, locker accommodation was provided on the ground-floor. But before this, the grey steel student lockers lined one side of part of the corridor on the first-floor of the main building, disfiguring it as only student litter can. But not from a student point of view: they domesticated themselves like cats in what the Principal

The memorial window above the central double staircase in the Home, depicting Joseph Cross and items of the textiles crafts below.

described as 'this funny old comforting building.' One evening a girl's voice pleaded to a little group: "Let's come and sit near my locker." Without the imagined need for recreational drugs they sat on the floor in companiable relaxation, the colours changing in the expanse of the sky to the west. This was when student numbers had so increased that the Principal, Mary Hamilton Wilson, dreamt of broom-cupboards and sluice-rooms being converted to educational use.

In the early days, residential accommodation could be offered to 50 girls and 3 teaching-staff as well as the Principal. The bedrooms (later used as tutorial rooms) were ample twin-rooms with a winding mechanism on a fan-light over the doors to the side-corridors. The Co-op furniture was solid: a double-wardrobe and a dressing-table with drawers. Before the students' arrival, bed-legs had been cut down by joiner / engineer Thomas Hooley so that the beds could serve as extra seats. The flower-printed cretonne curtains of Lancashire manufacture, inherited from the Home, were hung again at the windows by Matron / Housekeeper Mrs May Gardner. Some of the first-floor rooms had been dormitories for 3, 4, 5 or 6 persons. These were to be used as lecture-rooms.

In any residential institution food is a matter of emotional focus, particularly for the young. If the Ladies' sitting-room, with its double bay-windows, was the centre of peaceful concentration (it became for 14 years, together with adjacent rooms, the main college library, and later the reception lounge of Wyre Borough Council), it was the dining and recreation-room with its vaulted-ceiling illuminated by 8 stained-glass lights, and its pine floor, which was both the heart of the Home and of the College. It could cater for 200 or more, seated. The kitchen was adjoining through swing-doors, with space for conversion to, and accommodation for, self-service.

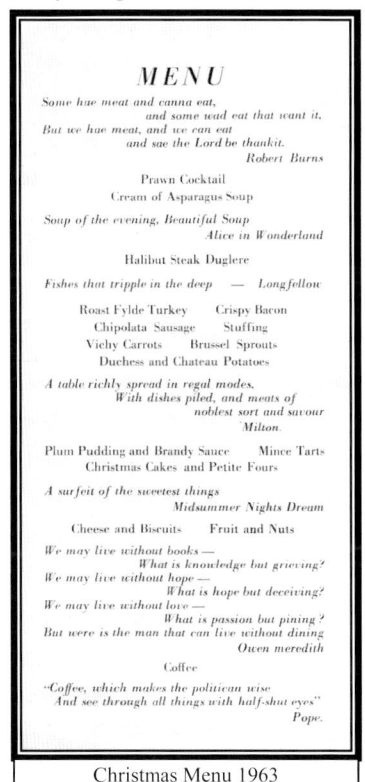

The kitchen equipment was all-electric and the late Superintendent of the Home had been heard to say that the fish-and-chip frying-range was the largest in Poulton. There were ample storage and preparation-rooms (including a walk-in refrigerator) with outlets to the north yard.

With so much space and scope, there was no difficulty in attracting a caterer – a Blackpool-trained chef. Within the education budget, Mr Vincent Darwen was a wizard. Using the superior refrigeration-room, he ignored the 'no use of left-overs' rule, a policy which assisted economy and added to the choice of menu. His Christmas banquets and celebration buffets would not have disgraced a five-star hotel of the time. They

---

MENU

Some hae meat and canna eat,
    and some wad eat that want it.
But we hae meat, and we can eat
    and sae the Lord be thankit.
                        Robert Burns

Prawn Cocktail
Cream of Asparagus Soup

Soup of the evening, Beautiful Soup
                Alice in Wonderland

Halibut Steak Duglere

Fishes that tripple in the deep — Longfellow

Roast Fylde Turkey   Crispy Bacon
Chipolata Sausage   Stuffing
Vichy Carrots   Brussel Sprouts
Duchess and Chateau Potatoes

A table richly spread in regal modes,
    With dishes piled, and meats of
            noblest sort and savour
                        Milton.

Plum Pudding and Brandy Sauce   Mince Tarts
Christmas Cakes and Petite Fours

A surfeit of the sweetest things
            Midsummer Nights Dream

Cheese and Biscuits   Fruit and Nuts

We may live without books —
    What is knowledge but grieving?
We may live without hope —
    What is hope but deceiving?
We may live without love —
    What is passion but pining?
But were is the man that can live without dining
                        Owen meredith

Coffee

"Coffee, which makes the politician wise
And see through all things with half-shut eyes"
                        Pope.

Christmas Menu 1963

were presented with quiet flair. Who could forget his lithe figure surmounted with its tall white hat in the dining-room carrying high the flaming plum-pudding? The 1960s was an era of cheap food and adequate student-grants. Mr Peter Long writes of him: "…unflappable, taciturn, invariably courteous, he was a remarkable man. Not only did he demonstrate daily that communal feeding is not automatically second-rate, but he kept within budget by such economical manoeuvres as buying in a large consignment of excellent tinned Christmas puddings in January, stashing them away, and serving them in the following June, dressed with brandy sauce, as College Pudding, to everyone's delight…" That was at the end-of-term party, making a good memory for the leavers.

The domestic staff, mostly Poulton residents, already had high standards in housekeeping and catering when appointed. They were well-managed by Miss Valerie Bennett (later to be Mrs Valerie Bateson) as Domestic Bursar from August 1963. Miss Bennett and Mrs Gardner, Matron, established the system of lodgings, requiring good relationships with the wider world, before the extent of the task justified the appointment of a Lodgings Officer, in the persons of first Miss Noreen Hunt, Mrs Winifred Suffolk, and later Mrs Brenda Stephenson, who stayed until the college-courses moved to Preston in 1983.

The hospital-style laundry, in a separate building beyond the kitchen-yard, was reputed to be able to deal with the washing of every housewife in Poulton. Its boilers were fired by electricity, and its walls covered in white tiles. It became a gymnasium and space for modern dance under the direction of tutor Miss Elsie Bond, and later Miss Enid Astin. A pantomime or two devised by students were also staged there.

However it was the 'living-in' start, the first intake of girls surrendering their rooms to the second-year intake, which established the college atmosphere of friendly care, student for student, staff for student. A remarkable tradition of tutorial help - drawing favourable comment from examiners - was particularly assisted by mathematics lecturer Miss Nora Usher and Mrs Sybil Cheetham – later Mrs Nawaliska – living in college from 1963, and making themselves available until very late each evening - giving support to students experiencing their first teaching-practice in local schools.

Continuity of Care

A view in the 1930's after Thomas Hooley had installed the porcelain basins on the front lawn.

A postcard from Poulton-le-Fylde

Amongst my Mother's collection of picture postcards, which she appeared to start in 1902, is one sent to my Dad stamped 'Poulton-le-Fylde' over the George V red penny stamp. The photograph is of the Joseph Cross Memorial Convalescent Home, with the clock under the hexagonal turret over the door at nearly 11 o'clock. The sash-windows on the varied facades are open. The spring bedding is set out in straight rows in the garden-borders, and neat triangular patches of flower-bed cut out of the spacious lawn; not a car in sight. The pencilled words on the reverse of the postcard say: "Dear Mr Bradley, thanks very much for the magazine, it was quite a surprise. I am feeling better and it is a lovely place, both the Home and the village. We are having nice weather. Yours sincerely, Nancy Pickup."

Mr Thomas Hooley – engineer – born 1901

But it is the flower-beds that date it before Tommy's time as engineer at the Home. The administrator at the Mary Macarthur Home for Working Women - further down Breck Road - lived next-door to Tommy in Garstang Road East.

Chapter 4

Continuity of Care

Tommy had been trained as an engineer, though he was then working as a Magistrates' Clerk at Blackpool. Mrs Dorcas Bury, Matron at Joseph Cross Home, told this man she wanted a fountain. Who could make her one? Tommy demonstrated his capability to Matron, went for interview at the Cotton Industries offices in Manchester, and was appointed as maintenance engineer. Soon the fountain, in white porcelain basins, was erected instead of the flower-beds as a further means of dissuading the convalescents from strolling and sitting on the lawn. Matron's house, off the picture to the right, needed the view exclusively she thought.

Both Tommy and I (as Librarian at the later College) were lucky to be here; so was anybody. Perhaps it was by 1933 that my unknown fellow-villager was 'feeling better' at Poulton. Thirty years after the postcard had come to my childhood home in Clayton-le-Woods, near Chorley, now on 5th June 1963, I was sitting on the wide doorstep of the Joseph Cross Home to start a job, to create a library and train students to exploit it. I waited happily for the handsome front-door, with its inset bevelled glass, to open.

The clock over the door, whose workings I was informed later by Tommy, were delicately balanced with a matchstick, told 8.28 am. I had caught the 7.53

steam-train from Preston. Far from feeling locked out of the job which was to last me through the next 20 years, I felt I had come home. Bees and birds were busy in the sun-warmed garden, now untended since the winter.

There was a quick trot within and a laughing little woman newly-appointed as Principal here from Keele University, Miss Mary Wilson, lifted my bag and led me through the revolving-door. Passing corridor-panelling of solid oak, I was led to a gracious room of agreeable proportions, furnished with a telephone and a large mahogany table. This table Tommy later polished to shine like glass on which "the cheapest food in Europe, which Britons then enjoyed" (a statement by politicians), was concocted into elegant dinner-parties by the chef-wizard Mr Darwen for students-in-training, neatly dressed for a special occasion.

Miss Wilson brought back to the room a smiling, broadly-small man with devil-pixie ears and dressed in blue dungarees. He quickly picked up my name and inquired about a connection with Whittle-le-Woods. He had been born there himself just across the A6 from the house where I appeared one late January morning, a generation after Tommy. He carried not only two potted schizanthus plants ("..or would you prefer something else?") but also an aura of zest in practical achievement and ingenious overcoming-of-obstacles, just like my Grandad Bradley. My Grandfather had lived at Church Cottage, Whittle-le-Woods, acting as an arm of discipline for the vicar at St John's during Tommy's exploratory and mischievous youth. Did the zest come from the water in Cow Well, to which we ran down a tower of stone steps after school?

So started a friendship based on the vivid memories of our happy, free childhood, ranging over the same loved ground. Tommy was not a swearing man, but he elaborately refrained from the use of any impure word in my presence, as he said my father had taught him at Sunday School.

After most of the other staff had gone to Morecambe, the building had been protected for over six months at night by Tommy and Mrs Hooley sleeping in 'Matron's quarters,' alternating with a painter named Bert Gibson. Now Miss Wilson was there alone. She had no feeling of creepiness, despite a fair crop of spiders' webs under the green night-lights gleaming down in every corridor on green rubber floor-tiles. In the small courtyard formed between the kitchen-premises and the corridor leading to the Georgian house, her own quarters, she thought it wise to have a circular iron 'lid' of a well firmly secured against student pranks.

Miss Scobie keeps Tommy

Miss Scobie, an officer responsible for three areas of education, higher, primary, and student-grants, administrator at County Hall (and whose duties on her retirement in the early1970s were distributed between three men) recognized the value of this embodiment of versatility, energy and experience. He was the maintenance engineer who had tended the building during the war when labour and materials were scarce. Miss Scobie herself had explored every corner of it with him. She was determined to keep him, and placed a few stumbling-blocks in the way of his going to Morecambe.

She let him try it for a bit, travelling tediously by bus. Then she said: "Don't let anyone boss you!" and offered that he have a two-week holiday, then come back to Poulton on an enhanced salary.

'Petticoat government' again? Matron Bury had gone, but was a memory; in many ways he had enjoyed the drive and colourful humanity of a woman-boss. It was said that she had been Matron of a workhouse and she was 'hot on discipline.' In this pre-feminist world, a woman of natural authority and personality could spread. If she had bulk, energy and entertainment-value, like Tessie O'Shea (then frequently on Blackpool Central Pier), she was accepted as a phenomenon in nature. Matron Bury commanded like a general on a battlefield, her blue nurse's cloak lined with red, flurrying out behind her, as broad as it was long. Those commanded employed the self-protection of deception as Miss Mary Wilson, Principal, discovered. This was before the retained employees realized that there was no need for fibs and evasions under a liberal regime.

The Building

The front door had been planned to be on the south-wing, with access from Derby Road. But a Mrs Brigsbury and her more gentle husband (whose hobby was carving ivory) owned the large house next 'up the Breck.' Mrs Brigsbury did not wish her view to be encroached on by this hospital for working-people. The *Cotton Industries Board* spent £100 (multiply by about 60 to find the present-day value) on the erection of girders on an iron-framework so she would not see anything except the chimney-pots. This fence remained until the end of the War. After threats of legal action and delays, access was re-planned to be from Breck Road, where it is now. That is why there were two exterior clocks, and two revolving-doors, a luxury in the 1920s. Tommy said that the present front-door entrance was never really finished. But there was some celebration when access was sufficiently achieved to drive in an Austin 7 car. It was driven the full length of the main corridor; it could not get out of the double-doors at the west end, and had to reverse back out again. Without practical purpose this was high-spirited bravado.

JOSEPH CROSS MEMORIAL CONVALESCENT HOME, POULTON-LE-FYLDE

Interior finish
The pride in good workmanship was seen in solid oak panelling lining the main 8 foot-wide corridors, and in the large oak surrounds, the double doors and the window-sills. The locks on all the doors (outer-doors and bedrooms alike) clonked into security at all times with sound keys.

There was *Vita* glass (the name now granted enduring status by a John Betjeman poem, *The Dear Old Vicarage*) in the large south-facing bedrooms. This was promoted as admitting ultraviolet rays, helping depleted adults and weak children to thrive.

Tommy's weekly jobs as engineer included checking the fire-hydrant and swilling out the man-holes. Every Saturday morning at 11am he checked the clock where mains water entered from the Breck, to ensure there was no leak. The water-tanks on the roof had enough water to last four days, even when the mains water was turned off. The pressure was such that it roared into the baths and WC cisterns like Niagara Falls.

The oak furniture in the Boardroom of the Home, which descended later to being the lecturers' common-room, was stately. The chairs ranged round a large rectangular table with a larger armchair at its head, made at the CWS Cabinet Factory at Broughton. The college library was later granted use of the matching leaded-light fronted bookcase, mounted on drawers and under-cupboards. It had retained its label which read: *'Designed: Poulton; Maker: Booth; Fitter: Rowson; date sent out: 16/9/30.'*

It seemed to have been presumed that the Board members would comprise of men exclusively, as from the room there was a convenient door to the lavatories, some of whose wall-mounted equipment would generously and audibly flush, even when there was no-one there. This was rather spooky for Miss Wilson when she was alone in the place, until she privately explored the noise and discovered the cause. This too-convenient door was bricked up, as the noise had too much entertainment-value for the lecturers relaxing in the common-room.

A colourful legacy to the College: Matron Dorcas E Bury
A flamboyant style was not lacking in Matron Bury. Having achieved (via Tommy) her fountain on the front lawn, she asked that another be devised in the refectory. She had her sights on a Winter Garden effect. Tommy pointed out to me a little recessed brass-pull near the great leaded-light window where he had accessed a hydrant to make a fountain. This gracious room, where the dances were held weekly had a good polished floor. The average length of stay for the convalescent was two weeks. Tommy said it was grand to see those who had sat round the edge listlessly on their first Friday evening, dancing on the floor the next Friday. He was a very willing Master of Ceremonies at the dances.

Brass
Tommy was willing to indulge Matron about fountains, but NOT brass. She collected ornaments made of it, elephants, candlesticks, etc, ranged on a high shelf in the 18th century house which, upstairs and downstairs she claimed as her quarters. It had been physically attached to the main hospital during building. On Fridays, two girls used a whole tin of *Shinio* polishing these, over 100 pieces. When she had other jobs for the girls to do, she pressed Tommy into the task. He complained to Sir Andrew and got permission to invent a mechanical-polisher. He broke one or two pieces and put them in the bottom of the basket, so he was allowed to do the brass only twice.

Pets

Matron's pet-collection included several cats, a Pekinese, and a black Labrador dog. There were budgerigars in cages, and goldfish in a glass-bowl for which Tommy made a special table. Even so, the cats had the fish out more than once. Chickens were kept on the 'Fleetwood end' land towards the old railway-line. Turkeys and two peacocks were added to the duties of care of the one gardener and the porters.

Gardening and painting

The gardener, Jack Uttley, propagated annually 1,200 wallflowers and 1,200 antirrhinums for the borders. Jack, who died before the War came, was allergic to tomato-plants and chrysanthemums, and as the season advanced could not open his eyes.

There was much painting to be done, so it was decided to have a permanent man. The Trades' Council at Blackpool was approached. The painters' union was informed of it, but it never seemed to get any further than the secretary: he decided the job would be for him. He was Arthur Tyler, not a young man when he arrived, and Tommy said: "Out of puff going downhill!" as he stayed so long in his job. It was a safe job, not vulnerable to trade fluctuations.

Arthur evoked the terrible wrath of Matron when he broke the glass in the clock-face over the front door. The wrath was calmed by Tommy making another glass and fixing it. There was a flagpole on top of the turret and when the rope broke, he climbed up and re-threaded it.

Matron required the ceiling of the laundry to be white-enamelled. Arthur was frightened of climbing. Tommy put planks up and went up with him as he knew he would be entertained. Arthur was always singing and could make up his own words to popular tunes. He had perfected the *'Max Miller technique'* of verbal implication, stopping before the 'improper' word, and leaving the sequel to the imagination and the laughs. No blaring paint-spotted radio needed to be on the planks with them.

The War – 1939

One Friday in October or early November 1939, there came three-days' notice to clear out all residents and staff. Everything changed. The government took over the building to be run as an 'infectious-diseases hospital' under Lancashire County Council. Mrs Bury stayed on, and Tommy, now nearly 40 and

experienced in St John Ambulance work, did any job that came to hand to make the place function. Matron Bury destroyed all the records of the Convalescent Home and applied her gifts to the new regime. A man named Carey 'from down south' (Hastings) came. He was a glazier, painter and decorator and 'pushed himself in' until he was 'nearly in charge of the office.'
The water-tanks on the roof were increased so the Hospital could run for 7 days without mains water. The diameter of the ball-tap up there was 18-20 inches, its arm as thick as Tommy's wrist.

A full-time night watchman was appointed. On his night off, Tommy, the painter and two porters did night-duty and had the following day off. All, the two painters, two porters and Tommy, worked a 44/46-hour week.

The first batch of patients admitted were evacuee children, some coming from as far as Caton, Lancaster. The average stay for rubella was two weeks. This is the infectious illness also known as 'German measles' for which the MMR vaccine (late 20th century) gives protection. The second batch were Air Force personnel from Squires Gate and Weeton. After the retrieval of the Army from the Normandy beaches in 1940, all civilian patients were put out, and about 120 soldiers came. After a wash and a shave, they slept for days. They just needed nursing-care, though some had contracted dermatitis from dirty field-blankets as they awaited rescue.

Deaths
A baby in the first batch of patients had died. Then one or two airmen died. Their coffins were taken out of the back-door at the 'Fleetwood end' of the main corridor.
Tommy laid out the dead (a senior female assistant, next in rank to Matron, 'finished off' the women); he did this as part of his job as an engineer, but he was paid extra for these services. The (now convalescent) RAF personnel thought it would suffice to shoot the coffins of those who died on the upper-floor down the iron fire-escape staircase. Tommy insisted on good order with the use of a rope at the top, and a man going down in front of the sliding coffin.

He told me somewhat mischievously that the last person to die in the hospital died in the very room I used as a Library office (it is now the Mayor's pantry), a room flooded with south light, with many brisk people coming and going.

Also, that a shed had been built as a morgue under the trees across the garden, which was the view from the window, a large rectangular lawn, bordered by trees to which the return of the rooks on winter-evenings was a noisy and cheerful event. Some went to the trees round St Chad's church, some to these 50 year-old sycamores. One year there was excitement as an owl reared its young there. In the rough grass underneath, bluebells, some white, some pink, appeared in the spring.

At one time when the hospital was full, Tommy was everywhere, going from room to room. Infection seemed to be multiplying, so members of staff were sent to Victoria Hospital, Blackpool for tests. On the way home, Tommy had a nose-bleed in St Walburga's Road, where the occupants of a police-car recognised him from his magistrates' court days, and brought him home. But not for long, as he had been found to be a 'carrier.' He was sent back to 'work' to go to bed in isolation. He chose to be in the very room, later the downstairs Library Office, where Mrs Hooley would be able to come and see him at the window.

In this diphtheria epidemic, ambulances lined Breck Road, sometimes stretchers were carried in the front door with a baby at the end of each. When Tommy had achieved two negative tests out of three for clearance, he would do inside jobs. The patients included one or two Dutch sailors, a WREN or two, RAF from Weeton, and a young Dutch girl in isolation because she had a skin-disease. She was lonely and distressed with the shame of it, so Tommy said: "You won't be lonely, I will give you a knock 4 times a day….and you may have a mate tomorrow.."

Christmas
Medical Officer Dr Hall came from County Hall from time to time. There was the usual scurrying round to tidy the place for a senior medical man's innocent eyes. But Dr Hall was too quick and noticed some 'pin-ups' being removed, and said: "Can't I see the boys' pictures?"

He noticed other interesting things too. Christmas was approaching, and ideas to make it memorable for the children grew out of the religious service held every Sunday by sister-in-charge. It was in the alcove at the centre of the main corridor from which the double-staircase led.

Chapter 4 Continuity of Care

At Christmas local people were generous. The painter-come-office man from Hastings suggested the staff make toys from spare materials, 6 of everything, including aeroplanes which Mr Carey painted. They were laid out when finished on the billiard-table. On request, an extra one was made for Dr Hall's grandson.

There was an old bath-chair remaining from the Convalescent Home days. Tommy was asked to build a sleigh on it. Mr Carey, a big man with a big voice which he deepened, took the role of Father Christmas. He wore large wellington-boots covered with silver paint. The old rocking-horse was refurbished with a new mane and tail. The sleigh-bells jingled (with hospital fire-bells brought into play) and Matron, behind the scenes for once, played a carol on her concertina as the sleigh rolled out of the billiard-room towards the children in the entrance-hall after breakfast on Christmas morning.

Tommy and a porter dressed in white gowns with pierrot hats, pulled the sleigh round the corner to the main corridor. It was loaded with pillow-cases bursting with toys bearing the children's names. So towards the alcove at the foot of the central-staircase, where an upright piano had been placed. There was singing and playing with the new toys until lunch. There was a Christmas lunch for the staff when the children had had theirs.

Other enjoyments
Matron's temperament was more fitted for peacetime enjoyment than war-time stringency. She had a petrol-allowance for her Buick, a powerful car first manufactured in 1904 at Flint, USA. Sometimes the children were brought to the hospital in it. Musicians with their instruments were ferried too. Matron herself 'could play any musical instrument; she was not supposed to mix socially with the Service people, but she did play hostess to them. She threw coins into the army cars so the personnel could buy a drink. That was increasingly her own pleasure. When she instructed her driver to go to the pub for whisky for her, he added half water to the bottle, and drank the extra himself. "Took to drink during the War, poor lass…" said Tommy.

Physically, her double-jointed arms presented rather a problem, when after enjoying the whisky, on two occasions she rolled down the staircase in her quarters to the door of the Boardroom. The Principal of the College, whose quarters they later became, noticed a large hook in the ceiling over the bath. It had been fixed by Tommy to hold a hanging-chain to assist the heavy Matron to rise from the water.

She still exercised authority, particularly over fire-practices. She picked the most awkward times for them, and if the spirit was in her, could call two in one day. If she saw Tommy and the painter emerge from their workshop together after the alarms, she would say: "…and you two keep separate…"

Air-raids
When the air-raid sirens sounded (they might occur twice in one night), Matron, Sister-in-charge and whoever else (of the two staff-nurses and 12 other nurses) were on duty, led as many of the patients as they could to the shelter under the floor, where beds were in readiness. Access was from the west (Fleetwood) end of the main corridor.

The War ends - and afterwards
Matron Bury continued at the Home after the War, with the help of Mr Carey, the man from Rye. Both retired in the February of 1960. Mr and Mrs Myers became Superintendent and Matron at the Home in the last couple of years, and supervised the transfer of operations to Morecambe at the end of 1962.

Down the Breck from the railway station.

A lively young generation of teachers-in-training would plaster the bedroom-walls with pictures of the Beatles. Tommy shortened the bed legs so that the 50 or so girls who 'lived-in' could sit on the beds. Some of the domestic-staff stayed on, together with Bert Gibson, painter, Joe Ward, porter, and of course, Tommy Hooley, engineer. All gave smooth human continuity. The rooks coming to the trees with their raucous cries might have observed the changes, but they still made their homes there every night.

Some recycling
The large oak surrounds of the fireplaces were dismantled to make more room for class seating, their fine wood used by Tommy to make cupboards and shelves. The corridor oak panelling and windowsills still gave luxury and the clock over the front door kept good time.

The sick-bay sited in Matron's old quarters was rarely used, rather an excess of vigour invaded every corner of the house and grounds. An old outbuilding of the farm, the near neighbour of the college beyond the Jubilee Arch, was a fine place to channel some of the energy. The students named it The Shippon and held their entertainments there. Even when a fine multi-purpose building was erected in its place, the name lingered on. Matron Bury would have enjoyed the parties, though the dancing-style might have been beyond her. The spirit of enjoyment was everywhere.

I thank you Joseph Cross, and also Miss Scobie, for arranging the human continuity so that young folk could flourish here, and I could be happy in the place for 20 years.

At the Helm: Two ex-Service Academics

Lieutenant Colonel M.H. Wilson. Allied Control Commission: Education Branch, 1946 -1950

We have recorded the influence of Mrs Dorcas Bury on the Home as a social institution. The influence in personal terms of the first Principal of the College must be similarly crucial. In the 1960s, before edicts of central government and reliance on information technology had not eliminated so much personality, it would still be felt that '…an institution is the elongated shadow of one man…' as R W Emerson wrote.

One could not know Mary Hamilton Wilson without knowing, or knowing of, her nephews and nieces (some with 'great' in front). We are grateful to Mrs Ann Borland of Newmilns, Ayrshire, for assisting with the following facts and for the family's permission to record them.

Before I warily submitted myself for interview for the post of Librarian, I investigated. A young assistant curator at the Harris Museum, Preston, a former student at the first post-war university established at Keele Staffordshire pronounced enthusiastically "..A grand little woman – Scottish…" She valued ideas and energy in all staff and students. She herself had been thrown after graduation on a labour market when jobs were scarce and had done anything that was offered in different schools.

I did not then know, when I was called back to the small interview room near the front door to be offered the post, that Mary Wilson was born on the 8th February 1912, the daughter of an Ayrshire pattern-maker, whose clear drawings were esteemed and used in the engineering works - Glenfield & Kennedy of Kilmarnock – even after his death. I knew little about the pattern-making trade, but it seemed to my ignorant eye that you had to be able to imagine materials inside out. Observing his daughter at work in her administrative role, it seemed to me that this was her way with human material. Turning things upside down, she wanted to know 'why?' and encouraged teachers-in-training in the detached point-of-view about people's personalities and attitudes. About herself, she said: "I could be a loud, organising Scot, so I

Chapter 5   At the Helm: Two ex-Service Academics

try hard not to be..." When confronted, she could easily change tack, see the force of one's argument and laugh disarmingly (she laughed easily) and say: "You know what I'm like!" She wanted to get things done and knew that creative action could be best achieved by giving people responsibility based on trust once their talents and attitudes had been diagnosed.

When for the purposes of this record I had typed some paragraphs about her, I sent them to her nephew, Archie Borland, and his wife Ann in Ayrshire. I had not met them, but Ann's generous phone-calls during Aunt Mary's long final illness had kept us in touch. One August morning they drove to Higher Walton from Southport where they were holidaying. It was a delightful meeting, seated in garden chairs, bottles on a table, the conversation expanding on the background to Aunt Mary's colourful family life. In the bag handed over to me was a 200-page typescript in a student's clip-folder whose contents had been disclosed to no-one. Her house in Sorn being cleared as she went into care, the script was in protective hands.

Aunt Mary with great-niece Janie Borland in 1965 outside the 18th Century House which was joined on to the "Home" building.

After racing through it myself, spellbound, I showed it to the Archive Librarian at the University in Preston. He agreed about its value. A bound copy is held there now at Class 943.0894/WIL – WILSON, Mary Hamilton, 1912 – 2001. *After the War was over: Memories of the British Control Commission in Germany* (1952). A copy was also supplied to Keele University Library.

1946 – 1950: Education branch of the Allied Control Commission

From lunch-time chatter, we knew our Principal had during the years 1946 to 1950 served in the education branch of the Allied Control Commission, and we could imagine the physical deprivations of that time. But she tended to report only the comical anecdotes. Her rank was Lieutenant-Colonel and she wore a blue uniform. Mesmerized by the animated scene after the boat had drawn into Antwerp she realized belatedly that the call for 'one red colonel' referred to herself, and that she was holding up the disembarkation. So she had to trot down to shore carrying her red VIP ticket watched by others waiting on the crowded decks. From such harmless incidents we knew that this woman, whose personality had formed the background to our college lives, had an active past not fully revealed. She did not talk about her faith-shattering experiences in that job, but never subsequently did she choose to travel in Germany. Her appreciation of an open society was reinforced by first-hand experience of the consequences of Nazi self-delusion and suppression, and her constant aim was to build an open society in our own small, privileged institution at Poulton.

Kilmarnock in the 1920s had given her sympathy with scrappily-dressed, under-fed, culturally-deprived children who attended the evening entertainments and lectures at the Institute, but the 17-year-old girl who set out from the port of Leith to Hamburg in June 1929, during her studies at Glasgow University, would experience what happened to people who were being gradually deprived of mental and moral freedom.

Mary's unpublished book
As a build-up to the later years working for the post-war Commission, Mary selects incidents which give ominous warning even in her first school-placement in the idyllic forest environment of north-east Germany

Mary Hamilton Wilson
First Class Honours, French and German.
University of Glasgow 1929/30

where the cultivated Dr Breymann welcomed her to his staff in the English department of his Institute at Oker. He had spent many years in England pre-1914. But in 1934 Dr Breymann lay dead in prison, suddenly taken from his home by 'brownshirts.'

In 1933, Mary was at a placement in France. Her German friend Karl had sent her a desperate letter: "…Get me out of Germany if you can, I shall never have any success here…" It was assumed later by her family that this was the dark-haired young man whose picture she always had by her bedside. The family never met him, but in the early 1950s another friend, a Dutch lady, came to Scotland for a visit. Ranja Lawrenson said to them: "I owe my life to Mary Wilson – we were to be shot…"

During her practice in a German kindergarten in 1929, Mary had been drawn to the attitude of a naughty little boy who would not conform to the expected action of everyone doing ALL things together under teacher's instructions. It had been easy for the Nazi Ministry of Public Enlightenment and Propaganda to exercise control over every form of expression in schools in that atmosphere. Even the infant-schools did not escape. Spiky toys to harden the character and stories of the great conquering race were implanted to support Minister of Education Rust's philosophy that 'the whole function of education is to create Nazis.'

The British and American method of re-organisation made few rules. The only major one was de-Nazification, so new textbooks had to be made and school staff re-educated. Some excellent old professors and teachers could now come out of hiding. They must build a new national education system themselves and find a way out of regimentation, obedience and fear of criticism.

Many of Mary Wilson's duties lay in setting up whatever teacher-training could be mustered in the remaining shattered buildings of Düsseldorf, with its creaking infrastructure. She eventually established 16 colleges. Thirty years later a book was published by H Hamilton – ISBN 0241896371 (1978), edited by Arthur Hearnden. He edits the paper delivered at a gathering of educationalists, some not only having served in the Control Commission, but about what happened afterwards. Its title is <u>The British in Germany; educational reconstruction after 1945.</u>

At a time of national self-questioning in the first years of the 21st century, this book is salutary reading; one straightens one's spine. As contributor Trevor Davies writes of the time in Berlin without bridges: "...We seemed to have unconsciously become District Officers on the model of the old Colonial Service coping with what turned up..."
More troubles ensued when Berlin was split by the Russians late in 1948. An inspiring episode of that time is recounted in Arthur Hearnden's book. A certain Frau Dr. Panzer, who had been in a concentration camp and escaped, was responsible for secondary education in the city. Her headquarters fell to be in the Russian sector. Into a meeting where all the school inspectors were present a Russian deputy Military Commandant with a revolver in his holster suddenly stalked. He spoke with violence and threats. There was a stunned silence; it was broken by Dr Panzer's contemptuous reply. Strong words which decided the future of Berlin education. Later, she was asked by an eminent educator where she found the courage to do it. This lady had, after the liberation of her country, been funded for a few weeks work in a London school. She replied to him: "The courage? At St George's, East Stepney..." It was an insult to threaten to re-educate her in any other way. These were the sort of people Mary Wilson had mixed with and most admired.

Keele
In 1951 she had been appointed lecturer in Modern Languages Methodology and Women's Warden at University College of North Staffordshire at Keele, the first of such post-war institutions.
She always proclaimed she could not write, but early in this demanding job she found the time to sort her thoughts in this vivid and convincing account, and to clear her mind of the searing experiences which confronted educationalists in post-Nazi Germany.
As a somewhat isolated community of clever individuals, Keele University furnished Mary Wilson with a fund of anecdotes. Available as she was on site as resident warden, she was vulnerable to persons who had quirks of character and the unresolved adjustment problems of late adolescents.

Poulton
She had said to herself: "...when I have a place of my own I shall eliminate these at the interview-stage, and now at Poulton I wonder whether I have selected a bunch of mediocrities..." This was not so, and she knew it. The

college had a flying start with an intake of young people who seemed to have memorable personalities, some of them reared by careful mothers when fathers were away in the Services and who had themselves shared responsibility.

Official opening of Poulton College 24th. April 1964
Photos courtesy of Blackpool Gazette and Herald

Mr. Percy and Mrs. Lord; Miss Mary Wilson; Alderman J. Hull; Right Hon. Sir Edward Boyle, Minister for Education and Science; Mrs. Hull

A brass rubbing of a knight gives ancient dignity to the very new library in our 1930's building

Sir Edward Boyle complains that he did not get enough sand and water play when a child

Through the years, both at staff and student level, there were some high-flyers amongst those balanced people. One academic visitor watching the students carrying their lunch-trays laden with Mr Darwen's succulent meals, said: "What nice people they look." There was minimal illness of any kind, physical or mental. For problems that a brisk walk along a Blackpool promenade would not cure, there was always a sympathetic listening-ear. A 'personal tutor' system was soon implemented, every student having contact weekly with their own group of students comprised of persons other than in their main subject classes.

These students had assumed much responsibility in college Societies and sports teams during the past seven months.

Mary Wilson's administrative methods were feminine, but based on the acquisition of information enabling her to be in line with, or a step ahead of, the necessary power-groups who were jostling for advantage. She disarmed by a smokescreen of chat and trivialities, not minding to seem less astute than she actually was. This would put people off their guard; it was only the sharp look which was constantly almost disappearing in a laughing face that told the observer what was assembling and organising behind that eye which was perceiving information on which her next decision would be based. She claimed the right as a friend does to be told the truth there and then. This saved much time, especially in relation to the still maturing young adult. She gained thereby many confidences, but the remarkable thing was that during the chattering she never disclosed these to others, so she retained trust. They were valued as psychological information leading to a balanced judgement.

Chapter 5 — At the Helm: Two ex-Service Academics

The town

The apprehension felt by villagers about cotton workers of loose behaviour coming down Breck Road to the Home has been recorded. The Principal of the College was anxious to dispel any notion of student disruptiveness. She perceived that the four churches had full congregations, the leading citizens of the past had cleared the doss-houses from the edge of the churchyard,* and donated a quite extensive park and children's playground. The public houses were well supervised and the shops displayed goods of refined taste. The Town Hall welcomed the College; when attending gatherings there Mary Wilson became acquainted not only with the prominent, but with the ladies who served the elegant teas, her pleasing ordinariness of appearance, with dainty hands and feet making her immediately acceptable. She loved parties, and exploited the delightful relaxed environment of the college building not only for celebrations, but for problem-solving. She liked to present a Scottish-cum-Mothers' Union version of this: to have us 'put on a naice dress and have a naice tea.' In short, to make a point of repose in a milieu where national education policies and social conditions were changing fast.

* This now attractive passageway, bordered by quaint shops, used to be monitored by police and avoided by respectable citizens.

Spouses were always invited to staff-functions. A mainly male academic staff brought wives who had often had to adjust their own children to a new environment. They became friends of the staff generally.

A Deputy-Principal

Two terms after the first intake of students a Deputy Principal was appointed – Ralph H Eaton BA, BSc (Econ) with Diploma of Education from both Liverpool and the University of Toulouse. He came to Poulton from Crewe College, where he had been senior lecturer in the Sociology of Education.

His own post-school 'gap-years' were very extensive, some of this period inside a tank of the Royal Armoured Corps, which he joined in 1943. After Sandhurst he progressed in 1944 with the 4th Royal Tank east from the Belgian Ardennes, crossing the

Mr. Ralph Eaton came as Deputy Principal in 1964 from Cheshire County Training College, Crewe.

Rhine being assisted by amphibious transport. As he proceeded after Bremen to the Elbe, news broke in May 1945 that the Russians had arrived in Berlin, and on the 8th August the atom bomb fell on Hiroshima. There was now no need to train for the Far East. The army of occupation of north-west Germany extended geographical and other knowledge, later topped up by a diversion to north Italy for 12 months. Tito, Yugoslav marshal and prime minister, had seized Trieste from Italy. A puppet government had been set up and Trieste needed guarding. Also, the British Government, perceiving a threatening situation in the Middle East, required that the army be sent to the Suez Canal Zone to protect it. From there, Lieutenant Eaton was released in September 1947, to settle to book-learning, train for teaching, and become Head of Modern Languages in a London comprehensive school.

With imaginations stretched and with a circumspect attitude inculcated, men often found that they returned to institutions where women had shouldered responsibility in their absence. 'Petticoat government' could be congenial and interesting. The college working day was longer than most school days, and since expectations of domestic life were not yet adjusted to such a regime, most applicants for lectureships were men. The new Deputy Principal swiftly gained their respect, and they were rewarded with understanding of their varied contributions (experience of young families is relevant in a college specialising in primary education and there were soon three very young Eatons) and a furtherance of the Principal's attitude of trust, which fostered enthusiasm and innovation. Three women staff, who in these early days lived under the college roof, fostering the tradition of strong tutorial support to students in the evenings, knew they had an ally.

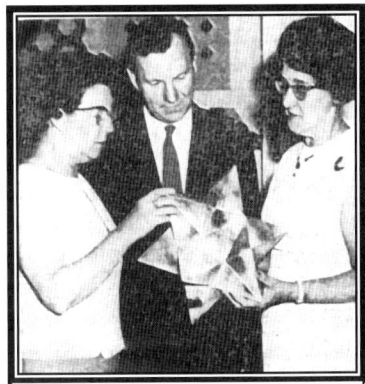

Miss M.H. Wilson, College Principal, Mr. R.H. Eaton, Deputy Principal, who spoke on college courses and Miss N.M. Usher, Mathematics Tutor, and Secretary for a conference in college. March 1967. Photo: Blackpool Gazette and Herald

Poised for Change

No ancient college could be more conducive to mental concentration and companiable interchange of thought than these few acres identified in the early 20th century by circumspect Trade Unionists. Round the varied range of gardens, and in the sparkling air, creative streams of energy seemed to flow.
Moreover, the Home building had been planned to receive the air, essential for mental health. The generous sash-windows opened above with cord-operation on a ratchet. Windows above the doors of rooms opening into corridors also had this ventilation facility.

Public transport in the 1960s was reliable. The railway-station at the top of Breck Road presided as a symbol of Victorian continuity and security. Many of the students in 1963 arrived and departed as had the cotton-workers - by train. Poulton platforms were constructed to accommodate 12 long carriages laden with visitors to the coast during cotton-town 'wakes weeks.' During the early 1960s, trains still arrived from Fleetwood with boxes of fish destined for distant markets.

Secluded from the west wind down a flight of steps, on the platform one stands or sits beneath a glass canopy in a peaceful dell where sparrows hop about near the door to the porters' pantry. On winter evenings a bright fire of best Yorkshire or Wigan coal at that period glowed in the waiting-room cast-iron grate, a long brown-painted bench seat on each side of it.

This non-profitable rail-route from East Lancashire to Blackpool, and Manchester to Blackpool was using up the last of the steam locomotives pulling corridorless carriages with facing cloth-upholstered benches, plus the occasional corridor-carriage.

One noticed one's companions on the 22-minute run from Preston. One morning, alighting at Poulton, I left behind in the corridorless compartment a man who had not moved so much as an eyelid since I boarded. His white downcast face was shaded by a light-coloured brimmed hat, pulled very well down, as though he had been dressed by someone else. He was a small flattened version of the passenger attired in white paper seated opposite Alice in Carroll's *Through the Looking-glass*.

Poulton Station, courtesy of artist Norma Wheatley.

My cousin, a GP in Blackpool, Dr Margaret Wignall, told me it was not unusual for an ambulance to be called from Victoria Hospital to collect these human arrivals deliberately loaded at Manchester by relatives who had no time for them. There was little provision for public care at that time. She said that GPs were financially recompensed for services to visitors , including these frail somewhat anonymous passengers, some of whom might live a little longer. It seemed to be quite a lucrative business, and did not cause serious trouble.

The old social order, too, was dying, and the newly-established college and its burgeoning life was to contribute to a quiet revolution.
Each of us has his own perception of social changes; I sometimes entered a train compartment at Preston where a lady from Leyland was talking to another.

They both alighted at Kirkham to go to the biscuit-factory – the Leyland lady secretly, not wishing it to be known locally that she had a job. One morning she was seated opposite me on the bench, leaning against the window, with one leg only on the floor as though getting out of bed, her loose-fitting light trousers adding to this impression. She looked tired as she usually did, and said with a scornful laugh, prompted by envy: "They went to tell him. He was asleep." She spoke of the Prime Minister, Mr Harold Macmillan, Edwardian, well-mannered and mystified by fibs in the Commons being explained to him by a young prostitute ("he would, wouldn't he?") and buffeted by winds of change blowing from Africa.

A few months after this, on alighting at Platform 4 one evening at Preston, I sensed some drama; why was Mr Patel, a businessman not long settled in Preston, and a regular reader at the Harris Library (my previous working scene), looking fixedly with admiration and hope in the direction of someone who had alighted from a London train? There, on the nearly vacated wide platform, wearing a pleasant public look, scarcely moving, as though giving time for onlookers to see him, was a small hatless figure in a light mackintosh. It was Mr Harold Wilson, first Labour Prime Minister since 1951 – though with a very small majority in the Commons. He had come to help deprive the long-standing Rt. Hon. Julian Amery of his Preston majority of 14. He achieved this in 1966: Labour was then elected by 2,418 votes.

Much later in 1975, one spring evening, news passed to a small waiting group on Poulton station that Margaret Thatcher had been elected Leader of the Conservative party. I was braced and interested, I felt a bit taller. The announcement reflected the full arrival of woman into a male enclave.

The 1960s had erupted 15 years before; food-rationing was even then just a memory, and there had been a decade of full employment. As the 1960s progressed, the Labour government supported the launch of the Open University, its liberating force assisted by massive media exposure. These innovations in higher education, leading also to Life Long Learning schemes in Polytechnics, etc, were urged on by lively academics such as Peter Laslett, Michael Young and Brian Jackson. They took sanction and shape under Jennie Lee, Harold Wilson's arts minister. There were grants for the higher education of mature students. A rich crop of fictional and other writing for children came to publication – a regular 'Golden Age' when books were cheap and provision in state schools more enlightened than at any time before.

There were to be various experiments in middle schools and comprehensive systems at secondary-level. These would eradicate the selective examination for 11-year-olds, which had resulted, so we were told, in a reinforcement of social class divisions, and which was the cause of anxiety to children and parents. For the next twenty years the Home behind the woodland frontage on the Breck was to assist in bringing these changes.

As I descended the gentle slope of the Breck on the 5th June 1963, my feet seemed scarcely to touch the ground. The air was light, the sun sparkling, and all was new to me. On the same footpath, bordered by spring garden flowers, I met a lady of late middle-age. She beamed a very kind leisured, friendly smile as though I were to be another villager whom she would meet again. No rush of traffic hurtled past us.

At midday I learned that the shops observed a civilised custom of closing for an hour. Richards' hardware store (the premises in the Market Square had been established in 1754), serviced by long-memoried grey-coated men who wore their detailed technical knowledge with reserve, kept this up the longest. The last Mr Richards in the business had started as a lad of 14. Decorum was retained during the closing sale in November 1979. Customers were admitted two by two, so that the usual courteous service could be given. It had been extended to Tommy Hooley when he worked in the 1930s for the Kendal Milne family at Singleton: at Christmas each year he was invited to go upstairs and select what he wanted from a range of mowing-machines, or other tools, of superb quality.

In Queen's Square, over the smooth mahogany grocer's counter, banked by towers of quality delicacies, Mr Reed's keen face shone with interest; his white apron wrapped entirely round a lithe body, he danced behind the towers to fetch a requested item from the cool back store. This was intimate, super marketing!

At 8.30 am, a ginger-and-white cat presided. He sat on the shop floor after night duty, ignoring us, but keeping an eye on the light-beams slanting through the shop door. These were the signals for intelligent living: other changes he would take in his stride.

Chapter 6   Poised for Change

In the Fylde some of these changes had particular significance. There were untapped sources of potentially professional labour. The administrative and management skills of women were exemplified in the Blackpool landlady. Her children absorbed an ever-changing social scene, and became self-dependent and resourceful. Now a college education was possible on their door-step.
Hitherto, without a local higher education institution, the wives of professional men had limited outlets for their energy. Now it could overflow to Poulton College.

Mrs Jeremy Gartside, having since contributed much to the reading and language service in Lancashire education system, and awarded a PhD in these studies, describes how she determinedly pushed at an opening door.
Her family was complete. At a cycling club, she heard that a mature man had been accepted as a student. When in 1965 this tall, 'thirtyish' lady was offered an interview, she expected something formal. But she was confronted by three laughing heads level with a large table. Mrs Sybil Nawalicka (infant education specialist), Miss Mary Wilson (Principal) and Mr James Booth (Course Leader, lecturer in philosophy of education, and wearing a bow-tie for the occasion) were seated on low chairs. In this atmosphere of a coconut-shy, so typical of the unrepressed humanity of the college, Jeremy 'threw her balls' successfully. She, together with Mrs Lilian Ellis, became the first of a substantial stream of mature women students. Many men too, without a local college, would have been beyond reach of full-time higher education. Memorable amongst these were the 'Knott Enders.' One former businessman arrived from there at 8 am, the habit of his working-life, to sit in the alcove at the foot of the double-staircase greeting people who arrived later.

In 1966, a second-year student aged 36 became President of the Students' Union. Another, Paul Greenwood, became the first full-time President in 1976. He was succeeded by a man (he stayed in the post for 2 years) who had had experience in the SAS. His power seemed to be in his mesmeric grey / black eyes, which struck fear. Did they really X-ray property and persons? A word to him and missing library-books vital to students' advanced studies re-appeared. He was worth 6 sniffer-dogs to us. He did not waste time on words.

Socially, these mature students, mentally flexible, contributed balance, tolerance and consequently humour, to the whole institution.

Eight locally recruited mothers, students at Poulton, received B.Ed Honours degrees at Lancaster University in July 1977.
From left: Elizabeth Cooper, Barbara Cartwright, Judith Coleman, Rita Walsh, Patsy Nelligan, Val Holdsworth, Joan Williams. Sandra Hartley (not on picture).
Photo: Evening Gazette.

Our Ally – France

The teacher-training courses were validated by the University of Manchester until 1967, when Lancaster University, then established in new buildings at Bailrigg, assumed responsibility. All students chose a main subject and a subsidiary subject as well as the compulsory education-course elements.
There were very few colleges which offered French. In the state primary schools, the occasional Roman Catholic school might teach a little French, but otherwise no child had the opportunity of learning a living language other than its own.

Miss Mary Wilson, Poulton's first Principal, when a lecturer at Keele, had been involved in an experimental pilot-scheme for teaching French in primary schools in the early 1960s; it was initiated by the Department of Education & Science. The British people too had to learn to look towards Europe, and towards our ancient enemy and modern ally, France. In January 1963, President Charles de Gaulle vetoed Britain's application to join the European Economic Community with a resounding "NON!" an attitude which prevailed until his resignation in 1969.

Poulton College's riposte to that was to host, only two terms after opening, a national conference of Her Majesty's Inspectors of Schools dealing with the pilot-scheme in primary school French. These senior people did not disdain to 'sleep in' during these days of the Easter vacation of 1964. The ample bedrooms, still uncarpeted but inspected by Miss Bennett, domestic bursar, to eliminate too much evidence of student occupation, were quiet, and no hotel plumbing could have surpassed the rush of hot-water into the large porcelain baths at the end of the corridor sprigs. Early morning tea was offered, carried into each room on trays by domestic staff, who wondered whatever they might be required to do next.

The various library and teaching rooms displayed the extensive range of books, slides and other visual-aids used in French schools, which Mr Robert Davies had brought back from the student excursion to Paris only a few weeks earlier. On his necessary visits to the University at Manchester which at that time validated our courses, he had also identified texts of modern French literature of which our library came to have the best collection in the North West. Together with a range of relevant objects and pictures, all these made a very attractive colourful display, not only drawing comments from the HM Inspectors, but also, especially after their use of the language laboratory, adding further sparkle to the eyes of children brought in from the Blackpool schools, this being one of the areas taking part in the national experiment.

Mr Davies, already very experienced in teaching at secondary level, had had to acquaint himself with teaching younger children as well as mastering very quickly the Tandberg Language Laboratory. As he demonstrated its use to all the academic staff, he said: "It's like driving a car – you have the skill but you can still go wrong…"

Lecturer Robert A. Davies supervises 12 booths where stuents work individually in the new language laboratory; or he can teach collectively from the console.
24th. January 1964. Blackpool Gazette.

An account of the student excursion to Paris was published in the college magazine *Breckan* Volume One – No 2 (1964). It is written by a memorable student Scott Berry; I shall quote much from it, as it conveys the spirit of the time. I know that if he bounds up to me concerning copyright I shall enjoy every minute: his personality jumped over every obstacle to human contact. I hope that if he had a long career in teaching, that his intense *joie de vivre* - like that of a highly articulate and intelligently bouncing dog - survived the oppression of the 1980s' bureaucracy in the profession.

In the early 1960s, the majority of our population now venturing 'across the channel' were 'innocents abroad.' Scott's piece conveys the uninhibited manners of the young of a country whose parents had not lived under domination of an occupying power in the recent war.

Chapter 7 — Our Ally – France

The visit took place just three spring-times ahead of the 1968 disruption of Paris by student rebellion about conditions at the Sorbonne; campuses in the western United States had even more violent troubles.

After boarding a bus in Blackpool on a drizzling March evening, and a Channel-crossing with Beatlemanic schoolchildren, the following day the Poulton party took a boat along the Seine and raced each other down the 1,000 feet of the Eiffel Tower. Scott writes:

"…It was while we were regaining our breath that a young man approached us carrying a strange weapon which proved to be a portable tape-recorder. He explained he was from Radio France and wished to interview us for a broadcast, and asked us why we had come to the Eiffel Tower. After several faulty starts I managed to explain that the weather was fine. After a long period of silence, interspersed with weird noises of hilarity from my two companions and sounds of bewilderment from me, I managed to tell my assailant that the sun was shining. After several nerve-racking minutes we gave up and the young man disappeared in search of some other unfortunate victim…

Our next experience came after a tiring yet interesting day at Versailles followed by an evening at Le Globe – a Parisian music hall. At 11.30 the performance ended and we were making our way to the Métro when Mr Davies and Mr Stone noticed a dance going on until the early hours of the morning. We decided to go and were glad we did! It was here that we really left our mark on Paris. Everyone was 'twisting' merrily when Sue Watkins and Dave Oldham began to do 'the shake.' Several Parisians gathered round showing both surprise and interest. So at the next 'twist' session we all did the 'shake' and soon nearly everyone on the dance-floor was gathered around us, the clapping being ably led by Mr Stone. The French dancers could not believe that we English did such a dance. Thus we had shattered their image of us….it was a tired and somewhat bedraggled party which arrived back at the Lycée at 8am – just in time for breakfast….that afternoon, after a morning in bed, we spent a very interesting time at the Louvre, where we saw amongst other treasures the Mona Lisa. Unfortunately the Museum authorities must have got wind of our visit, for the Venus de Milo had been shipped off to Japan for safety…"

And so back to work. Mr Davies reports: "The French department also acquired in that first year the *Voix et Images* audio-visual course, which we were able to use in another experiment. This was the teaching of a foreign language to <u>all</u>

Poulton students irrespective of their choice of main subject. It was also used to teach senior British Aerospace executives to enable them to deal in French with their counterparts in Toulouse...."

The college was subsequently asked to organise a conference similar to the one for HMIs followed by several methodology courses for teachers of French in Blackpool primary schools.

Six-week exchanges began in 1964/5 between Poulton students (main French level) and French students in *Écoles normales,* the first link being with the town of Moulins in central France.

The following year saw the introduction of innovative integrated subsidiary courses instead of individual subjects. French formed part of the Integrated Humanities course alongside English, History and Religious Studies.

College French Society artistes welcome Mr. Arthur Leslie (Jack Walker in T.V. Coronation Street). From left: Mr. Eric Plant (compère), David Hunter, Josephine Kershaw (secretary), Kenneth Field, Mr. Leslie, Judith Waugh, Anthony Gray, Philip McGoldrick, Michael Antrobus (president).
Photo: Blackpool Gazette and Herald.

French was the first subject to be given permission, after a visitation from a team from Manchester University, to start the BEd degree; heretofore, a Certificate of Education had been awarded. It began in September 1968, by which time the department had four lecturers as well as Rob Davies, including Peter Edwards, Alan Godfrey, John Rhoden and Barry Preston.

Local mature students with family responsibilities valued this nearby opportunity to graduate as did local teachers who could upgrade their qualifications with the BEd, and so enhance their salaries. Students who had graduated from other Universities were admitted to do a year's Post-Graduate Certificate of Education course. So, from 1970 there was intense activity on the campus with every corner of the old 'Home' and College House used by the 500-600 students and staff.

In 1975, Poulton and Chorley Colleges merged with Preston Polytechnic (the Harris College so designated in 1973). The last teacher education courses entered Poulton in 1977, to complete their BEd degree in 1981.

A new BA degree in Combined Studies added opportunities for lecturing full-time for many Poulton staff, and in the case of French, on Bilingual Secretaries courses, Interpreters' courses, BTEC courses, and BA in European Business and Languages. So Mr Davies' continuous years of service ended at Preston as Foreign Languages Co-ordinator in the Faculty of Business and Management, whereby in 1990, the Languages for All courses enabled 1,020 students to choose a foreign language as part of their degree-course: "…a repeat experiment," as Rob Davies writes, "although more elaborate, of one carried out a quarter of a century earlier, at Poulton-le-Fylde College of Education…"

Amongst the BA students of those early years studying French, were Mr Leonard Ganley of Blackpool, who in his 70s took in his stride the pressures of presenting written work on time, and of adjusting to being a student in France.

Mr Brian Baker of Fleetwood, integrated superbly during his year abroad and found a French wife. He had a delightful ironic humour. Evacuated from a Manchester school during the 1940/41 bombing, he had made an earlier cultural adjustment to St Mary's primary school at Bamber Bridge, and the discipline of the cotton trade which included clog-iron inspection on Saturday mornings, and the weekly bringing of the disinfectant from the Council Offices.

The progress and personalities of these men were a daily pleasure to the library staff. The library had expanded to the large prefabricated sheds then, so Brian sat looking from its picture-window with a view to Fleetwood and to his *alma mater* - the ICI plant at Thornton.

Native French Speakers
From the beginning of these courses, a native French speaker was appointed. These attractive young people were as different in style and personality as we think we Britons are. Two of them found a spouse at College. Bernard Penin married Gillian Mallett, Assistant Librarian. His career was in England. Their two children were able to attend the French primary school in London, the only one offering such fully bi-lingual education in the country.

Developing Artistic Talents

From its founding, two art tutors – not one only as for other main subjects taught – were appointed at college, denoting that at least it was understood that the joy of sensory experience underpinned a young child's development.
The senior of these tutors, Miss Christine Holmes, writes: "Art education aimed to develop the students' own visual and creative sensitivity, as well as their understanding of children's artistic development and expression. Practical work for <u>all</u> students in a wide variety of media aimed to make students adaptable, practical and inspired in the classroom…"
Modern embroidery in the 1960s, in its use of varied materials colour and design, gave a free rein. Young ladies no longer needed to complain of having to 'in fading silks compose Faintly thi' inimitable rose...' (poem: *The Spleen* by Anne Kingsmill Finch, who died in 1770). So it was not long before the upstairs corridors, for the first time since the excellent plaster had been smoothed in 1929, were hung with arresting fabric-collages and creations in thread.
Miss Holmes remembers Mary Wilson's peals of laughter when she had offered this new tutor, on arrival, a room full of bedsteads and mattresses, and another with bed-pans and medical paraphernalia in tiers, before she rushed on to establish (above the former men's recreation-room) a science laboratory. This was by government edict: no educational institution could be without one as we attempted to catch up with the Soviet space-research.

The other tutor appointed was a potter and sculptor. The 'Home' architect had had an expansive perception of accommodation for motor-transport. The large roof-lit garage became Mr Brian Stone's pottery and sculpture studio.
Very visible from the Principal's entertaining-room was the front yard which soon became strewn with carvings and large pieces of driftwood, metal objects and rocks, enthusiastically scavenged from Lytham St Annes beach, and brought back in the college minibus.
Mr Joe Ward, in his grey dust-coat, a very popular character, one of several staff that 'came with the Home', managed to be in manner both sunny and laconic. Instructed by Miss Wilson to reduce to order a litter of mixed metal pieces he would tolerantly lift these strange shapes saying: "That's a Knight of St. Columba to Mr Stone…"

Mr Stone enthused the students, so college tradition and freedom for creativity attracted another good potter when Mr Stone left in 1968. During Mr Bryan Trueman's era, facilities and expertise developed to a level that on entering the main foyer, one was astonished to see in the glass display-cases worn old boots and leather satchels – tawny with much use. Surely not? The human pottery creases, the tones of clay as matured by living, made an arresting image of the beauty of ordinary things. Also one was, on most days, welcome to view the studio and to share the soothing stimulus of pots being turned on the wheel, and the excitement and surprise of the varied contents of the cooled kiln.

A "Poulton-le-Fylde News" photograph of students at work in the pottery department at the Poulton Teachers' Training College. Friday 22nd May 1964.

Bryan Trueman stayed with us until 1975 when he was offered an attractive post in Australia. Labour Premier, Don Dustan, had been elected in 1967 and the Adelaide Festival became not only the state's, but the nation's, pre-eminent cultural event. It became a haven for artists and intellectuals – a multi-cultural fraternity - perhaps offering a more intense experience of the open society which prevailed at Poulton College. Returned to England via Grange-over-Sands, establishing a studio at Farfield Mill, Sedbergh. He set out again in 2006, for Australia, photographs of his wonderful work still being on the high seas.

Christine Holmes left in 1969 to become Vice-Principal of Bath College of Home Economics. She had been 6 years at Poulton. Other talented contributors to the Art department were the late Warren Farnworth, Terry France, Peter Peacock (who in 1971 exhibited abstract panels, big as doors, in the Poulton County Library gallery), Mollie Picken, Gifford Rolfe, and the late David Hill. As well as his wittily-observed paintings, his laconic wit remains in the memory.

As college activities spread and space shrank, we became more territorial. A geography tutor, infiltrating a library-room with his display-materials was imperturbable: he would not budge. It was one of the very few occasions when, protecting library-space, I sought the Principal's help, saying: "I could get no more response from him than from a currant-bun!" Just then David Hill put his

Chapter 8   Developing Artistic Talents

head round her office-door, and hearing Miss Wilson's amused reaction said: "No, a plain teacake!" Beware a painter's eye!

The students

Christine Holmes writes: "Those taking Art as a main subject specialism developed very strong individual talents in painting, printmaking, textiles, fabric collage, embroidery, or in pottery and sculpture." Gill Tomlins, who arrived in 1963 from Cheshire, lived in a room in a side corridor off the main spine, near the Library Office (which is now the Mayor's Pantry). She covered all her half of the shared room with photos of the Beatles, which after three months disappeared completely. She was one of my own personal tutorial group (for pastoral care) and I noticed how all this first-year intake of girls, especially Gill, set the tone of helpfulness to those following on.

Gill Tomlins, on completion of her course taught in local schools. Pictures of the Beatles were replaced by beer mats in 1964 on her half of her college room.
Photo: Blackpool Gazette.

Christine Holmes writes of Gill studying Primary Education, Art and Textiles: "She had a unique creative talent and a gift for working with children, which I feel was innate rather than developed by the college. She went on to become a brilliant teacher in local schools. Despite immense family support (she had married and had two young children) she died of leukaemia very prematurely; a great loss to the teaching profession. She was the most talented student I ever worked with…"

Exhibitions of the students' and Christine Holmes' work were mounted in the new County Library at Poulton (whose opening in 1964 was a longed-for event) and at Lytham St Annes Art Society annual exhibition, in the Lower Hall of Lytham Baths.

Miss Christine Holmes at the exhibition of art work done by third year students. Summer term 1968. At Poulton County Library.
Photo. Blackpool Gazette.

All the primary schools used for the two spells of practice (which all students undertook) must have glowed with the free use of colour and shape inspired by Christine.

The Performing Arts

Two college subjects which particularly linked town and gown were Music, and Religious Studies. The two tutors who brought mature social and intellectual energy came in 1965 and departed in 1979, due to the winding-down of the BEd courses taught at college, and the unimaginative approach of the adjudicating authorities to modern Religious Studies as a component of the Combined Arts degree. The Polytechnic at Preston to which we were now fully affiliated regarded music as a hobby interest.

When Miss Mary Wilson arrived at Poulton in autumn 1962, she found Poulton churches with full congregations. The Methodist church had raised enough funds for a new attractive building nearby the 19th century Congregational church, both on the other side of the shopping-area from St Chad's – a neighbourly arrangement. St John's RC church, school and social centre is opposite the trees at the foot of the Breck. All were quietly welcoming for artistic and reflective pursuits.

When Mr Denis Brooks, musician and educationalist, noticed the vacancy at college, the Principal said to him: "I don't know why you want to come here, there's nothing going on musically." Only one student had opted to study music as a main subject. Perhaps the college building and the open south door of St Chad's church had much to do with the decision of this highly-qualified man. Perhaps it was crocus-time. Mr Brooks moved his family into a house opposite the college gates.

Things happened in good order. The town itself was expanding. The church needed an organist and choirmaster, which became another outlet for Denis Brooks' energies. When the Rev Derek Whitehead came to the college department of Religious Studies, St Chad's needed a curate. He was himself musical, so until summer of 1979 these two appointees pulled together.

Some of the happiest memories for 1960s children will be Mr Brooks' Saturday morning school at college, burgeoning into the Fylde Academy for Young Musicians. Later, Lancashire County took over the classes, running them at Hodgson's School and attracting 350 young people.

Chapter 9   The Performing Arts

A Saturday morning Music School at College. It met a great need. Mr. Denis Brooks initiated it. It burgeoned into the Fylde Academy for Young Musicians held at Hodgson's School.
Photo: Blackpool Gazette.

The late Miss Dorothy Smith heard of this in its 'baby' state, and came to help voluntarily. When lecturer Mr Robert Long – musician and composer – left college, she was appointed to the vacancy, and stayed until there was no place for musicians on Polytechnic courses.

Even before the free-standing fine hall with a stage was built (this £62,000 building starting in summer 1969) memorable concerts and 'dramatic events' were presented either in the refectory, or in one of the larger rooms. One of the first productions by the students' choir - augmented by one or two staff – was Karl Orff's *Carmina Burana* in the former men's billiard-room.
In March 1967 Mair Jones, harpist with the Liverpool Philharmonic Orchestra, brought her precious golden instrument to an event in St Chad's. It was the first

of many such visits, when a college choir of 50 performed Faure's *Requiem* and Britten's *Ceremony of Carols*.

In July, a newly-formed orchestral group accepted the Methodist church's invitation to give readings and a musical evening. This became an annual 'going down' event.

In March 1968, Haydn's *Creation* was performed at St Chad's by the orchestra college choir with three soloists drawn from local professional talent. Britten's *Cantata St Nicholas* was presented in the college refectory, local schoolboys taking part. Christopher Biggs was guest tenor soloist. Also in the programme was Eric Rowley's *Miniature Piano Concerto* with student Jennifer Brennan at the piano, tutor Robert Long conducting.

At Christmas, a concert in the refectory included unaccompanied songs for the small choir conducted by Miss Margaret Lee; the full choir gave *Toward the Unknown Region* by Vaughan Williams.

Friday 6th. December 1968 students rehearse for the Advent carol service in the college refectory.

After the usual Christmas concerts of 1969 and 1970, Advent at St Chad's saw its east end filled with the, now large, college choir to perform *Messiah (Part I)* and Britten's *Ceremony of Carols*. In March 1971, Hodgson's School was packed for a full *Messiah* including Olive Dewhurst and George Allen as soloists. The college year ended with an inter-denominational service at St Chad's, conducted by Fr Baron from Kirkby Lonsdale; congregations from the four main Poulton churches being present.

In the Easter term, Hodgson's School hosted the choir to perform Britten's *Simple Symphony* and Mozart's *Requiem Mass*. In November 1978, Denis

Brooks' last major orchestral concert in St Chad's included Handel's *Organ Concert No 1,* and four centuries of orchestral music from Orlando Gibbons to Peter Aston.

Fate ordained that two artists, still with much to give to the Poulton scene must, in 1979, give their notice to the Polytechnic in Preston: Rev Derek Whitehead (now PhD from Lancaster, having submitted his dissertation on the doctrine of intention in Anglican theology), lover of English words and drama transmitted through the Anglican liturgy and the pulpit: "St Chad's has the best acoustics of any church I have preached in, you could drop your voice anywhere," and Denis Brooks, who had given so much to music in the Fylde for 15 years. Both must seek new pastures.

Dance, drama and speech
One of the very first members of staff was Miss Elsie Bond. She was appointed for Physical Education; her background and experience was ideal for the training of teachers of both young children, and early adolescents. It was the *Laban* school of dancing that had most influenced her, the natural movement and expression of emotion in the body. The creativity it encouraged led to personal development. It was pleasant to watch and could be presented with words and music. Forty years later, in 2003, it has been found that 'compulsory dance' such as this up to the age of 14 helps, boys particularly, to develop confidence in relationships and other forms of school-work.

When Miss Margery Manifold was appointed to the English department for speech and drama, there was co-operation between these two enthusiasts. Without a stage and the usual aids to 'suspension of disbelief,' Margery produced a fully-dressed *Noah* in the college refectory, overcoming many obstacles – some of which were turned to dramatic spectacle when the animals approached through the auditorium from the main corridor.

When the alternative courses were established – of five terms' duration replacing the traditional subsidiary courses – there were many original presentations of dance under the direction of Miss Enid Astin, both in the refectory and in the gymnasium (the former laundry) such as *Winter* – interpreted in dance, jazz, lights and poetry.

The Performing Arts   Chapter 9

When we saw that mathematics featured in the branch of these courses labelled 'creative,' some of us reached for the encyclopaedia, as we had not advanced to that stage of study of the subject where creativity is recognised. The humanities and environmental course did not need to jerk us into lateral thinking quite so much as in creative mathematics.

There were poetry and prose readings in the large college room where tatlers and spinners had played billiards. The acoustics and intimacy were superb. One remembers excerpts from *King Lear* with Gerald Battye and mature student Len Bolton, both men whose exuberant personal style we had associated more with comedy.

Students whose more modest language arts needed development were sympathetically assisted by Miss Manifold, not only in bolstering confidence in the classroom, but in presenting their own recital in the gracious college room - projecting a shared pleasure in English words. Sometimes the release of their personalities seemed to be magical.

From the early days there was an improvised stage at term end in the gymnasium, and here the students produced their pantomimes, with invitations to families in the town. Publicity in the local press was excellent.

In June 1964, Mr Peter Long, Head of History, shared his passion for drama with the college Dramatic Society, greatly assisting the production of *A Phoenix too frequent* by Christopher Fry.

In December 1967, English tutor Arthur M Gill produced Shakespeare's *Twelfth Night* at Hodgson's School, the school pupils being present on the Friday matinee. All the cast were college students and tutorial staff: Rev Derek Whitehead was a very frisky Sir Toby Belch, and Peter Long a very hard-used Malvolio.

Religious Studies

Nearing retirement, Mr George Holroyd gave the department a noble start. He was associated with the Methodist and Congregational churches in Poulton. In 1967, Rev Derek Whitehead, already on the staff, took full responsibility. It was a time, just after the Beatles, when youth culture, with its own clothes, music and money, began to be the force it still is. 'Flower-power' and pop-groups in massive rallies infiltrated hallowed ground at such places as Glastonbury. The formal traditional study of religion did not present much glamour to the young.

The selection (from 37 applicants) of Mary Wilson as Principal had taken note of the broad integrated curriculum she had helped to pioneer at Keele; this had a breadth appropriate for teachers in junior schools, in which Poulton's teaching in these early days was to specialize. Compulsory alternative (to one's main subject) courses were launched for all students, with a certain amount of choice. Religious Studies did not recruit. So the Rev Derek innocently suggested introductory lectures. The result was that more students applied for his subject than could be handled, to the disgruntlement of colleagues who talked scathingly of Derek's 'song and dance act.' His course took some of their best students. In 1965, one of Poulton's very first two mature (over 21) female students was offered Religious Studies, not her chosen study, but Rev Derek's lectures were so exciting that she adjusted to it gratefully.
The parishioners and visitors to St Chad's church could hear his sparkling persuasive gifts from the pulpit in that 18th century nave in which, he writes: "...it has the most perfect acoustics of any church I have preached in. You could drop your voice anywhere..."

Student numbers led to another tutorial post being needed. Serendipity had a hand in the appointment of a lady who was already fulfilling the role of 'lodgings officer' having moved to the Fylde to her mother's home. Dr Noreen Hunt's academic background was impeccable: a Driver Research Scholarship by the Council of Royal Holloway College enabled studies resulting in a PhD dissertation, published by E Arnold in 1967: *Cluny under St Hugh 1049-1109*. She herself had been taught by inspirational teachers - amongst them Dom Knowles, author of the 3-volume *The religious orders in England* (1962). Noreen Hunt remained with the department until 1973, when she became the

Vice-Principal of Bede College, Durham, making one of four Poulton tutors who, after gaining experience at Poulton, moved to such influential posts in larger colleges.

St. Chad's church at the heart of the market town.
The present building dates from the late 1700's though there was a church here since at least 1094. Mr. Thomas Hooley told the editor that the sexton, long – serving in the early 29th. Century, brought extra crocus bulbs with the gratuities from visitors grateful for his help. That is why they are so prolific.
Photo: Valerie Fillingham. Poulton-le-Fylde Photographic Society.

Immediately John Ewan and Peter Curtis, newly-appointed, brought complementary gifts. John's travel on the Indian sub-continent gave first-hand experience of eastern religions. The Lancaster University syllabus (which was now followed) gave particular attention to the nature and content of Hindu scriptures, and the encounter between Hinduism and western thought in the 19th and 20th centuries.

Institutions in Preston, both Muslim and Hindu, became our friends. Colourful and arresting were visits to Poulton classes of gentle young Hindu girls, performing their symbolic dances in brilliantly jewelled robes.

Advances in these studies had been so rapid that a knowledgeable visitor proclaimed that Poulton library stock outstripped in quality that of similar colleges in the north-west. Also, the high quality of the tutors of these subjects was perceived (with some envy) by Dr Harry Law, Director of the Polytechnic. However, Religious Studies subjects as devised and taught by these 'academic ornaments' (as described by Dr Law), were not accepted as a component of the new Combined Arts degree. The modern library stock was accepted by Lancaster University Library and our tutors soon found outlets for their talents elsewhere, but they made a strong team, and much was lost.

It is one of the ironies consequent on hasty political and bureaucratic decisions that at the end of the 20th century the study of theology and religious subjects attracts students at university level. The new university at 'Priest's town,' with its Hindu temple (itself offering learning opportunities) and its many other institutions, could have fulfilled this need very well. Poulton College's 'academic ornaments' would have given such courses a flying start.

Coming Out in the Professional World

Such a supportive and delightfully varied (for walking, swimming, boating) natural environment offered much to the maturing young adult. There was contact with city theatres and cultural events by coach excursions.

But what about the professional development? What profession, other than teaching, would generously incorporate into their working day whilst shaping the progress of their classes, the invasion of raw, inexperienced late adolescents on 'teaching practice?' Yet teachers do this with grace. In the Fylde, in Blackpool and in some cases in Preston schools, they did it with style.

The variety of venue was a great advantage for the college. By the time the students were allocated a school, Mr James Booth, the very able leader of the Education department, had held many consultations with his staff, and they with their students. Their education tutor was present with subject specialists over a period of a month, when there was dialogue on how to teach that subject in Junior school. The students participated in the discussions. All shared in lectures with extensive notes given in Mathematics, English, History, Geography, Religious Education, Art & Crafts and Environmental Studies.

In early College years, the Nursery / Infant students were taught mainly by Mrs Sybil Nawaliska, assisted by Mrs Agnes Connaughton and in later years by Mrs Betty Wilkinson. Both had a child-centred approach. Sybil's living quarters in college were open to any students who needed support during teaching-practices. She, by patience and encouragement, helped one young man to unfold a special talent with 'upper infants.' A rapport with young children is often difficult to 'diagnose' in the maturing adult, but an expressed wish to teach is usually based on some instinct, which needs guidance and opportunities. Norah Usher, Head of the Mathematics department, also 'lived in,' so there was close liaison in their joint curriculum work, Norah too making herself available late evenings.

Dr David Foster, a man of great achievement in the education world subsequently, and an historian, writes of his own apprehension on entering an infants' class, where one of his subject specialists was 'placed.' Tutored by

Chapter 11   Coming Out in the Professional World

these two indomitable ladies, and later by his own three children, he looks back on his nervousness with amusement.

Local experience of schools gave the college staff skill in placing students. The sea-coast and entertainment industry makes a child tough and articulate. Some of our students at great former Board Schools (such as Revoe Junior School) faced classes which might include at least one amiable aspiring stand-up comic with an ample support from side-kicks elsewhere in corner desks.
I was not, as Librarian, a teaching practice tutor, but a student of our second year intake wished me to share her enjoyment of her lessons at Pilling C of E Junior School. Welcomed by the Headmaster one winter day I sat in the afternoon music lesson and the story lesson, experiencing all the competence and love of children which led this student later to long service in the Fylde schools. After pioneer work as Head of Roseacre Junior School, Blackpool, Mrs Doreen Burrell retired in 2001. She was just one of the talented Poulton students who more than fulfilled their potential.
The Headmaster issued another invitation to Pilling for the 1966 Christmas lunch. Cooked on the spot from locally produced ingredients, the rural serenity seemed itself out of a storybook. I was able to take our newly appointed Assistant Librarian, Gillian Mallett. Gillian herself, later Mrs Bernard Penin, had a very responsible career in school librarianship.

A third source of assessment, as well as the two college tutors, on final teaching practice, was the external examiner brought in from another college or university.
The benefits were two-way – the expertise of local teachers to our students and the injection of new ideas from college staff and the opportunity to discuss school problems.
George Ellison writes: "In my own case I had close links with Revoe Primary School Chess Club, which had over 40 members. For some years I gave an annual simultaneous display versus the children and about 4 members of staff, including the Headmaster, Tom

Chess champions. George Ellison to the right.

Mayhew. I had a warm welcome on subsequent teaching practice visits. [G D Ellison became Fylde senior champion of the Blackpool & Fylde Chess League, an institution which endures still after the college closed.]
In 1975, Fred Clough was appointed to college, a great strength to Poulton Chess Club.

Students have expressed appreciation of the value in school to them of the support given by the college's Environmental Studies department. Geography Studies had a long future at Preston Polytechnic and the University. It was well-placed at Poulton to explore the varied geological strata of Lancashire. There was also a dedicated team originally grouped round Rural Science, the long-standing enthusiasts were Phil Doughty and Geoff Roper and their henchmen, who at all times of year ran a small-animal department in one of the sheds on the back land. They kept guinea-pigs, hamsters, rabbits, mice and rats of a certain breed. Some of these could be loaned to schools and visits were arranged to college - enjoyable tours conducted by the students, who welcomed the children they had taught at school.

The Poulton Elk

National headlines and much excitement was made by a much older local animal. In autumn 1970 thanks to the alertness of Mr. Tony Scholey of Blackpool Old Road, Highfurlong there was much excitement for local scientists. Brian Barnes, biology lecturer was one of the team that recorded the find of the Ice Age elk and ensured that 'Horace' is in the permanent collection at the Harris Museum Preston.

Brian Barnes biology lecturer. He co-operated with Ben Edwards, Tony Stuart and John Holloway, all specialists in their field. They agreed that Mr. Scholey's find would enter into the literature of early life all over Western Europe.

A museum curator demonstrates the size of the elk and the barb which stranded it in the swamp. Photo. Blackpool Gazette 26th. September 1970

Chapter 11   Coming Out in the Professional World

Lessons on plants, and respect for all living things were assisted by the college gardeners. A very old greenhouse was pulled down. Ken Abbott, propagating gardener, having produced wonderful border and indoor plants from it, left and was succeeded by Arthur Gardner and a new larger greenhouse further west, whence some of the more portable and child-friendly products could be taken to school. Arthur's personality conveyed patience and humour; this and the aroma of the greenhouses were a great source of refreshment and interest on Open Days and to all of us. The lawns and flower-beds were always a joy.

When Mr Charles T Evans was appointed to the college staff in 1967, the playing-fields behind the main building became very busy with team games, and via these, links with the community, already forged by the Students' Union, were extended by him. Football was played in the local league, and there was rugby and mixed hockey against local teams.

Basketball was played at Kirkham Prison, and before Poulton swimming-pool was opened, the baths at Kirkham were used. Students helped at the annual Lancashire County Council regattas, and schools' sailing events at Tower Wood on Windermere. There was camping at Coniston, and students assisted with sailing, canoeing, fell-walking and climbing.

Charles Evans' outdoor skills added much to Combined Environmental Studies courses, and to Geography fieldwork.

Preparing to sail from Tower Wood Outdoor Pursuits Centre June 1977

74

Coming Out in the Professional World   Chapter 11

Students sailing on Windermere. June 1977

Poulton students skiing in Scotland in the 1970s

Chapter 11 — Coming Out in the Professional World

Malham in West Yorkshire 1977

Grappling on a Lake District route. 1979

Coming Out in the Professional World   Chapter 11

Looking towards Fleetwood, showing the extra two acres bought from British Rail in 1967, extending beyond the large new greenhouse, accommodation for animals and the Environmental Studies shed

Women students are using the tennis courts of "Home" days for varied ball practise in winter.
Photo: Poulton College.

Living

When college was first established, car-ownership by the young was unusual. This factor, more than any other, fixed the social atmosphere. We became a resident institution where bonds were established in shared living space, meals and public transport.

The welcome into local lodgings was voiced early. A lady wrote to the Principal in 1963, to say that her own family now being themselves away at college, she would be glad to offer an informal family-atmosphere in her home. A good start. But in 1963, most first-year girl students, about 80, could use the former Home bedrooms down each sprig off main corridors, with luxurious baths and hot-water at the end. Wardrobe and drawer-space was ample. Men (14 students) lived in the annexe above the council offices in Lockwood Avenue, nearby.

At the end of the first year, girls moved out into lodgings, approved by the Lodgings Officer, making room for the new intake. 'Hostesses' were required to provide 'bed and breakfast,' with access to a warm room where their tenants could study in peace and quiet. College was open all day and at weekends for meals, lectures and relaxation.

'Hostesses' received little remuneration from Lancashire County Council, but many insisted on providing a snack at suppertime and help with laundry and other tasks.

Mrs Win Suffolk, who took over responsibility from Miss Noreen Hunt as Lodgings Officer, writes how much she was supported by Miss Val Bennett, Domestic Bursar, and Mrs May Gardner, Matron. Difficulties, few as they were, could be settled by discussion, or fresh lodgings were found. "…many friendships were begun and lasted through the years…" Nearly 40 years later, Win meets hostesses in the Poulton streets who remember the days of college with pleasure.

When Mrs Brenda Stephenson took over the Lodgings Officer job in summer 1972, she assumed the same pastoral and diplomatic role as Win Suffolk, and corroborates her comments about the general welcome. She says some ladies in early widowhood with a nice house took on a new lease of life when their housekeeping skills helped these intelligent young people to settle away from home. By this date there were 385 students in approved lodgings, some hostesses receiving 4 students, some liked to have 2 men students. As in the early days, some hostesses were invited to eventual weddings and christenings. Remuneration weekly was meagre: about £3:6s:8d (£3.33) in 1972 for bed and breakfast, rising in September 1976 to £5.75 for a shared room with a retaining-fee of 75p per week. The Georgian house, Singleton Lodge, which is now a restaurant, could be reached by a late bus which stopped at top of the lane. Travel expenses could be claimed from County Hall. There were buses to Over-Wyre accommodation too.

During August vacation, 1983. Some staff who delivered succulent meals and household care. Mrs Brenda Stephenson – Lodgings Officer at top left. Assembled outside former Library offices to give Miss Bradley a good send-off to Preston Polytechnic with a beautiful water colour by Victor Hadfield.

In the late 1970s and 80s, students became interesting to the 'money-market,' and banks vied with each other for their custom. The Lodgings Officer aimed to persuade the students to sign for their term's lodgings-cost before the liberty of a chequebook (which most of the students had never had before) came into play. This was the 'pre- credit card' era, and cash was expected in shops. Debts were not a problem for the men's and women's college wardens, unless a rich parent, with a student unable to claim grant, refused to contribute any

Chapter 12   Living

expense allowance. Furthermore, if other charitable resources could be tapped, after a successful college career such students often had a choice of three school jobs.

After the change to contracts at 18 rather than at 21 years, student self-catering houses became popular. Entrepreneurs realised that tax relief could be obtained on second or even third mortgages gaining a good income from the rising house-market. In such accommodation, students rarely went to their parents' home, adding to their independence by a vacation job, spending freely locally. In that situation they had no right to come into college sick-bay if they were ill, though there were first-aid facilities.

However, the personal tutorial system Miss Mary Wilson had put in place was still valuable, small groups of students being assigned to a tutor for weekly (or other) meetings with other than their main-course tutor. As women's warden, Win Suffolk made use of this system for liaising generally to discuss points of view until in most cases an amicable solution was found.

Miss Mary Wilson's pastoral care was scrupulous. Brenda remembers that even in 1972, a very responsible student - after her year's residence in France as part of a four-year course, asked for her recommendation to overcome the Principal's wariness about her going into self-catering accommodation.

Until the library moved into the 'sheds' in 1976, the library staff from the main corridor could be witness to the most pleasant annual scene in college: the thank-you afternoon tea in the refectory for the hostesses. Wearing hats and summer dresses they exuded that benevolent sensitivity that mothers and grandmothers conveyed in those days, the smiling 'are they really doing this for me?' look when someone was taking trouble to do them a kindness.

The students themselves too showed gratitude by Christmas parties. For Christmas 1970, the Students' Christian Fellowship mustered a dozen or more cars and the two college minibuses to bring senior citizens to a concert and a meal in the refectory, decorated with streamers and holly. A film was presented: *Roses of Britain* with a song-sheet of old and loved songs. Students Ray Harrison and Chris Sanderson were at the pianos. There was also a college band group.

Smooth running of the domestic side was much due to many staff over-stepping job-description. Mrs Stephenson worked from 11 am to 11 pm on Sundays.

| Living | Chapter 12 |

> Setting out to Norway in the early 1970s
> Bryan Trueman, potter. Charles evans Outdoor pursuits and David Meecham geography, with David Longworth below, accompany trainee teachers. Was there a meal for them on their late return ?
> Photo Blackpool Gazette and Herald

Returning from a distant field-trip in the minibuses, it was not always possible to be back for evening meal-time. The tired travellers were catered for, Brenda phoned chef, Mr Darwen. She was directed to the great walk-in refrigerator for ham salad and all the ingredients for a refreshing meal.

Her knowledge of students' personal situation outside college was passed to the librarian if books were not returned on time. So one knew when to relax, when to accord extra liberties, or when (to use a late 20th century word beloved of politicians) to 'target,' which in our case meant using a student-neighbour to retrieve the volume by a surprise visit.

Chapter 13 — The Library

The Library

Miss Scobie, the County Administrator responsible for higher education, had chosen the pleasantest ground-floor room, formerly the ladies' sitting-room, for the Library. Two large bay windows look over the south lawn, bordered by flower-beds diligently tended by the newly appointed propagating gardener, Kenneth Abbott.

At certain times of the year, a hare enjoyed the turn of speed afforded by the tarmacadamed terraces. There were owls in the sycamore trees planted nearly 40 years ago; bluebells, some pink or white, bloomed beneath. The lawn was free from human intrusion except in some days of early summer when the revolving-door at the foot of the double-staircase was opened, and when we opened the glass-doors at the side of the library-room to give access to the stout garden-benches.

The Home ladies sitting room in pre television days: piano and wireless set

Students in front of the Library windows 1968, the lady 'Home' residents had been allocated this lawn privately

At the large tables in the window-recess and between the shelving, study facilities were excellent. People who opt for the teaching profession are not reclusive in temperament: the subdued noise of the corridor was companionable. The refectory was nearby, and social relaxation offered in the alcoves below the staircase and in the junior common-room. For the girls living in the corridor-sprigs those first years, it must have seemed like having one's own country-house library.

The variety of persons passing down the corridor, and their smiling faces, was a constant stimulus to 'deliver the goods.' In the library office next to the library, the activity of unpacking, classifying and cataloguing, contrasted with the supine occupants of this former bedroom (the very sick were nursed here), was very urgent.

The view from the library office window (now the Mayor's parlour). Thora, a library assistant came to us in the early days of College in 1964 from the Co-Operative Association Library at Manchester.

Advised by another librarian at a county college, Padgate: "don't let them (ie, the tutors) know how much money you have, they will be comparing their allocations to the last penny..." Forestalling trouble, I worked to give them what they needed when they wanted it, and made the money stretch. The second-hand bookshops in Dublin were marvellous. Just before I began at Poulton, I was passing through on holiday, taking Peter Long's lists of history, carefully put together whilst in his teaching post at Darwen. Climbing ladders, I found many basic texts in fine recent editions. My assurance that there was to be a new college was believed, and the parcels arrived, some bearing interesting book-plates of former owners, and bringing an aura of that city of scholars and writers to be incorporated into the Poulton College. Later we had our own book-plate devised by the late Warren Farnworth of the art department; it still enriches thousands of books in the University Library at Preston.

Chapter 13 — The Library

I took more lists to Manchester (Gibbs' Bookshop, in its cellar a particularly good quarry) and Liverpool to track down second-hand and out-of-print bargains, and to local library-suppliers. Holt-Jackson at Lytham, and Askews at Preston could not have been more efficient and helpful.

Supplementary collections of loans from the superb Lancashire Library were, in the early days, invaluable. I could call in the basement of County Hall, where it was housed in those days, on my way to the morning train and bring a bag-full, to be greeted with much appreciation by a tutor planning a new course. The inter-library loan system, particularly of photocopies of articles from periodicals, is one of the glories of service to scholarship.

The issue system for loans had to be 'do-it-yourself.' There was open access until the college doors were locked at 11 pm. At first I worked single-handed, so trust and recognition of individuals was the only control. Not as bad as Philip Larkin's situation in his first post as a raw graduate in a small urban district library at Wellington, Shropshire, which he describes in his essay *Single-handed and untrained.*

The library was respectfully, but seriously, visited by an Inspector about 8 years from the start. He identified about 12 books in the catalogue which were not on the shelves. Where were they? The next 20 minutes were a reassuring testimony in honesty in use of the issue-system, and of solidarity. Tutors appeared from their rooms holding valuable volumes. Word quietly went round to students to look in lockers. HM Inspector stood in the corridor. All items were accounted for; it seemed that our losses were less than the national average.

Though our communication system might seem to be at the level of a primitive tribe, it was rapid and cheap. Our recognition-game, played in a very mobile society, now becomes more difficult. I had noticed that as we began to recruit from different counties, that a certain facial type could be recognised, so I asked at induction that students add

4 library staff; Maureen Wilson, Joan Bardsley, Margaret Wild, Anne Bradley. The old greenhouse to the left.

The Library   Chapter 13

their home address to a slip which we filed, adding spare photos from the admissions office. Also strong fashion imperatives tend to make young people want to look alike. Men were easier to remember than the girls, though one's perception of a beard as a second-year phenomenon was thrown off-scent by first-years having grown them during the summer vacation.

By this time, the library had a small staff all as keen as mustard: we learned names as a teacher in class learns names. To be approached in the corridor by name, or even jocularly as 'Miss Bournemouth, ma'am' only a few weeks after arrival gives the impression that one is being noticed about the small matters on which library efficiency depends. The tannoy-announcement system in the refectory was the last resource, the Students' Union office giving willing assistance. It was based on the public exposure of the village-stocks system: the overdue short-term loan soon appeared mysteriously back to us, after the announcement. A year or two into merger with the Polytechnic, a small fine was charged on overdue loans.

Building a library from scratch is an exciting experience, one could say that each item was brought up by hand; to enjoy the experience of exploiting its growing contents in depth with students committed to their subjects and to help them improve their essay-grades, was a luxury. All the library staff, most of them long-serving, overheard the discussions, contributed to the search for materials and shared the satisfaction. When final results and degree-grades came on the typed lists, we rejoiced over them.

The rapid inflow of new books and periodicals was a stimulus to everyone. Whilst the library was in the main building before moving, after 14 years, to the 'sheds,' we displayed books newly on Fridays in the main corridor. They contained slips to reserve them by name.

Out of the 'Fleetwood door exit' to the library sheds.

Chapter 13 　　　　　　　　　　　　　　　　　　　　　　　　The Library

When Rural Science was studied, some unlikely student or staff names were seen on the slips in such texts as *Goat-keeping for Beginners*. People would stand together for some time inspecting and browsing. Mr Ron Jackson, tutor in education subjects, said this was a weekly treat for him and that the facility stood for what the college was about, the stimulus of new ideas presented in a sociable way.

The Derby Road housing scheme is now underway in the 1970's.
Mr. Thompson (Pleasure Beach), our good neighbour lived with his young family in a roomy unpretentious house near the trees.

The 'joiner's workshop,' where Tommy Hooley and later Ray Bradbury could be found, adjoining the gymnasium gave us immense support. An extra piece of framed pin-board for the simple display-system appeared rapidly. One much appreciated resource was the 'Coffin.' It was an 8-foot long floor-standing box with post-holes in the top to receive returned loans, for the library staff to check-off and redistribute. When we merged with the Polytechnic 6 years before the courses moved to Preston, this sturdy functional wooden object was the cause of hilarity there. In 2003, a sophisticated return to boxes has been installed at the University Library at Preston. These boxes are plastic.

Special collections
Courses exploring the local environment led to the assembling of a 'local studies' collection. During the 20 years of Poulton College, many private libraries were dispersed on the open market. By arriving very early to order by

phone, one could secure rare items. Halewood's Bookshop at Preston was also helpful. We were grateful to Mr Ellis Tomlinson, a local resident, for donations of back and current copies of the annual proceedings of the *Lancashire & Cheshire Historical Society*. This collection was available to qualified teachers who followed a one-term full-time course in local history.

The Conservative Association at Blackpool, when moving to other premises in the 1970s, donated a collection first assembled by a Mr Wainwright, which was valuable to us for its statistical material on 19th century trade.

Both these collections are in the archives of the University Library.

It was a pleasure to visit a Vicarage Road house in Poulton to select very interesting items from the private library of the late Mr Potts, an architect. I was assisted by his scrupulous, generous daughters.

Our collection of original texts and objects illustrating the history of teaching, proposed by Mr Peter Long and greatly assisted by our school contacts, is now in the care of the Judges' Lodgings Museum at Lancaster, in which the Museum of Childhood is incorporated.

Everybody's children as well as visiting infant and junior classes enjoyed the light corridors displaying things to read and the welcoming spaces of the college.
Clare Longton sits near the library shed with Anne Bradley in 1981, her mother Patricia, with most of the staff was relocated at Preston Polytechnic in 1983.

We assembled a special collection of modern books for children, and of critical histories loaned to students only for dissertations. A generous supply of children's books, and later of multi-media kits, was available to support students on teaching-practice.

Chapter 13   The Library

Three of the college library staff, one full-time and two part-time, achieved Open University degrees. The supportive atmosphere of the college gave all the library staff, confidence to do interesting, responsible work in the wider world.

At a time when young professional library staff were scarce, we were fortunate to attract from Bournemouth Gillian Mallett as Assistant Librarian, the first appointed. Only 23, she commanded obedience. Having married French assistant Bernard Penin, her career in England ended in 2004 at a sixth-form college for girls in Cheshire – before they moved to Yèvres in the Vendôme.

To the right: Assistant Librarian, Gillian Mallett, in 1967

Mrs Margaret Wild, who finished her professional career at a large college in Somerset, gave immense support at Poulton as Assistant Librarian during the 1970s, immediately after which she qualified as a teacher at Elizabeth Garnett College, London.

The Assistant Librarians Christine Worsley and Mary-Alice Monaghan displayed amazing equanimity during the anxious time before appointments were offered to them at Preston Polytechnic.

Two assistants, then part-time at Poulton, were taken aboard too.

1980's Library Staff.
Freda Lewis, Anne Bradley, Mary-Alice Monaghan, Patricia Longton and Christine Worsley

88

Visits, Visitors and Social Style

To see how other countries 'did it' was part of the educational experience in the 60s and 70s. There were visits by tutors to Dominica (British Council), Swaziland and Ghana. In January 1968, 30 Poulton students and 2 tutors were among 800 others on an educational cruise of the West Coast of Africa.

In 1973, a professor in the English department of Saginaw Valley State College in Michigan, USA, found he could claim funding to assist his students to have first-hand experience of British culture. Born and bred in the Fylde, Professor W L Whittaker explored his own patch, visiting colleges in Lancashire and Cumbria. He perceived the open happy atmosphere of Poulton senior common-room. Things were soon arranged. As one of his 20 students who came in the summer of 1974 wrote: "What we did for these first two weeks was to learn about a completely different way of life, and form strong friendships with Poulton students. We ate with them…went to classes with them, were included on their field-trips, drank with them in the pub across from school, and were drawn into their lives and circles as if we had been there all our lives…"

"Never before in my life," writes Buffie Alegaard, "had I seen people so warm and loving. Not only the students and instructors, but the people of the town were as interested and fascinated by us as we were by them…" She was amazed by the 'real meat shops' and the fish-markets, or a store selling only cheese or only fruit, and the milk-bottles waiting in front of everyone's door.

"…the town was so gentle that it amazed me how I could walk home five or six blocks at 11 pm after leaving the pub, and feel safe…the English are beautiful, and easy-going and happy. If I could say thank-you a million times for all they have done for me, it would not be nearly enough…" [*Herald Weekly* – p16 29th November 1974]

As well as trips to the Lake District and York, I suggested (somewhat dryly) a look at the 'real' Lancashire, backyards and mills seen from the East Lancashire railway-line to Colne. Landscaping and demolition has made it different now, but then it was the authentic Victorian thing. We in cars met the travellers at the railway-station and started walking from Laneshaw Bridge over the fields to Wycoller. As we negotiated each gate, some of the girls asked how far to walk yet? It is only 2 miles. They loved the little bridges and sat on them.

The small rooms of Haworth Parsonage Museum were less trying. The heads of the African- American men nearly reached the ceiling above the wall where the Brontës had scratched their first words on the plaster. They made cheerful, vigorous inquiries as to what all these folks had died of.

Fifteen people from Poulton were hosted by Saginaw College in 1976. Enid Astin, seconded from Poulton, was teaching Physical Education in Ohio at that time. She made the 500-mile trip to Toronto airport to meet not only the four pieces of luggage she had asked for, but to pile some of us into her car to take us the 15 miles to the city. She stayed with us for the long weekend sight-seeing, including the Niagara Falls. On the long drive in the minibus to Michigan, the initiator of all this, Leslie Whittaker, had the company in the forward seat of our Derek Whitehead. At the frontier where passports were checked Derek received a specially hearty "thank-you Reverend…" At other times he might sit at the back entertaining us on the long runs, sometimes in the dusk, by word-perfect renderings of Noel Coward songs. At Saginaw College he was invited to give a course of lectures; he chose *The History of the Church of England*. We were welcomed everywhere - at the 'borough' departments and a whole morning at the Police Station, where we learned that one must buy a dog-licence, but a gun did not need one. We were driven to Dearborn and the Ford Museum, to the one-time virgin forests to the north of Lake Michigan, and to the elegant spaces of the University of Michigan at Ann Arbor, where huge extensions to the library were planned. The son of my Australian host and hostess, from the Dow Chemical town of Midland, came smiling (a first-year student on a bike), the only bit of the place Derek said that looked like Cambridge, England. We realised how 'small-town' we were, used to garden-walls on which the coats of domestic animals had been rubbed for centuries. Kay Harley, of the Saginaw Department of English fixed everything for us, together with Leslie Whittaker, attended receptions with us at college, made introductions and drove us everywhere. Later, she enrolled for a course at Lancaster University, and together with her US fiancé, enjoyed sailing on the Lancashire coast. She brought 11 more students in 1977. A most satisfying friendship for all, widening cultural horizons.
Poulton's Tony Goddard, who had co-operated with the arrangements, passed our test for his future appointment at the Polytechnic in Continuing and Comparative Education with flying colours.

Three visiting students came from Hungary in 1973, and a party of 20 students and 2 staff from a college in Utrecht – with 12 more in May 1974. They came via Lancaster University, organised by the *Educational Exchange Council* in London. I notice from issue number 391 of the student newsletter PLUG that they were appropriately entered on the 25th June to a Dutch Euro evening, admission 25p plus one tulip, with Dutch gin liquors served by an all female 'Dutch' staff; Dutch goodies included Dutch cheese.

Three soviet students from the party that came to Poulton in May, 1977, with Poulton student Pat Kelly and Mr. Tony Goddard, organiser and lecturer in comnparative education. This visit coincided with the visit of 11 students from Saginaw Valley State College, Michigan.
Photo: Blackpool Gazette

Staying in Poulton homes, a group of women student-teachers came from the USSR from towns as widely apart as Volgograd (Stalingrad) and Sverdlovsk. Also in 1974 some came from Moscow - all very much under the discipline of their group-leader; no walking home without her after an evening out at the *Oak*. In 1977, a group of potential teachers of English came on a 5-day visit from the USSR.

In 1971 (or 72) our administrative methods in education were studied by a very courteous Japanese gentleman.

From South Africa a guest of the British Council, Mr C A Naguran, came in 1976. He was in charge of education-planning for the Indian community in the whole of South Africa. He reported: "A man might be a top surgeon there, but if he is an Indian he has no right to vote."

As hosts, the Poulton climate helped us a lot – there were no draughty outdoor walkways as on the eminence of Bailrigg at Lancaster University. Sheltered and sylvan, the grounds gave comfort for pleasant meetings. When the library moved to the 'sheds' in 1976, our invited visitors could be seen approaching across neat flagged paths, and arrived smiling usually after a good lunch. A very high-spirited group of mature men attached to the Lancastrian School of Management from Bilsborough Hall (then recently in public ownership as

Judges' Lodgings) followed the late Lord Derby, tall and urbane, into our simple but very cheerful accommodation as though we were in Court, or on stage: *'Enter lord and retinue...'* He signed the Visitors' Book 'Derby Knowsley.'

Perhaps the library at Bilsborough Hall was far more stuffy than ours – now in the 'sheds.'

The same spirit seemed to obtain in a party of senior Commonwealth visitors which the library staff greeted (we all made ourselves available for service in the large entrance room). I know I received an invitation to Benares from a tall Indian gentleman, with directions how to find an office on a 4th floor there, in very friendly fashion.

A liberal atmosphere of pastoral care welcomed visitors. As hosts, did we receive some spin-off from Blackpool's tradition of entertainment? Our neighbour beyond the 'sheds' was Mr Thompson of South Shore Pleasure Beach fame. His family was young and enjoyed the luxury of miniature motorised cars. We had excellent relations, so the sound of revving engines was limited to certain times. The noise was nothing compared to that of the pile-driver when housing was extended, on this once flood-prone land, in the early 1980s. One of the young library staff was sensitive to this, so I climbed over the moon-like landscape to inquire. The answer was: "This machine is very old and cannot help it."

Locking of the college main front door (the only door used late evening) was 11 pm. Until that time, a duty tutor was present, their location known to officers of the Students' Union. The 'living-in' girls in the early days of college could apply for a 'late' key. Having admitted themselves, the numbered key was to be placed in a wooden box neatly fashioned by Tommy Hooley. It was shown as a curiosity to the Chancellor of Lancaster University, Princess Alexandra, in the library during her visit (which she requested) to the exhibitions marking the institution's 175th anniversary. Intellectual development is claimed from Preston's Institution for the Diffusion of Knowledge established in 1828. How fitting that Poulton's contribution to these merging strands should include this charming little box made from Cotton Convalescent Home scrap wood, thoroughly seasoned oak.

Mr Ron Jackson, Senior Lecturer, who ably administered the teaching-practice system in school, acted occasionally as late-duty tutor. During the evening a young lady presented with a headache. He made careful note of giving her an aspirin tablet from the sick-bay, and was thereafter known as 'Sister Jackson.' Such, in those days of innocence, was our 'drugs scene.'

Pastoral care and supervision extended to areas of relaxation. When the 'New Shippon' was nearing completion it was arranged at the last minute that a small bar and a stage should be erected – a victory by Miss Wilson and Mr Eaton over bureaucratic obstacles. Profits from the bar were to be allocated to improved student facilities. Saturday evening dances in this free-standing building attracted youths and men from Blackpool. Trained in attitudes of responsibility, the Students' Union asked for help with a difficult regular visitor. Miss Wilson said: "Send him to me." After an informal interview in her nearby apartment, her pronouncement was: "He is not 'the full shilling.' Do not allow him in again." Considering that a violently-thrown chair caused the death of a by-stander at a dance at Preston Polytechnic in the early 1980s, such precautions seem now justified.

On one occasion the bar was closed, the room emptied but the visitors – at 1 a.m. – would not board their private bus to depart. The police had been called, but no law had been broken; they stood by. Miss Wilson came out; she wanted to go to bed. She soon reduced them to mesmeric compliance by unstoppable volubility. In short, she told them to go: they filed on board and went.
This was the frontal attack by hot liquid speech which she used at County Hall. One of her now experienced tutorial staff had been refused promotion because "…we have no remaining positions of that grade." When she arrived at the office in person, she heard: "…this man is a bachelor, isn't he? They don't need money like married men, do they?" After the full Scottish verbal assault, the speaker of this was reduced, with a quivering hand, to finding a spare position.

For younger people, Mary Wilson's approach was milder. In higher education nationally, we had sailed through the 1968 serious campus troubles; in Paris General de Gaulle was called out, and in the US deaths occurred. Not quite knowing how strikes were organized, our Poulton students whipped up some feeling concerning the right to have one more Saturday night dance per term. The strike was planned for a Monday. Ear to the ground as usual, Mary Wilson

Chapter 14 — Visits, Visitors and Social Style

asked the Men's Warden, the Reverend Derek Whitehead, to array himself formally, and she donned what she called a 'naice frock.' Neither of these representatives of authority entering the nest of sedition was physically daunting, but in the Students' Union, the approach was a shock. Handbag was at the ready. The surprise attack came: the bag was opened and drinks all round were bought. The action was reciprocated. By 10 o'clock, after much unstoppable merry chatter, the strike had dissolved to lectures again on Tuesday morning.

The fashion for strikes passed. Or were there other factors? It was usual for the Principal to attend the first dance after a new President of the Students' Union was elected. The new President, a student of Religious Studies, Paul Welch (at the century's end Paul became Rector of St Mary's, Pulborough, Sussex), told the Men's Warden that on the occasion of his leading off the dance with Mary Wilson she said firmly: "I'll lead!"

Spreading

A major alteration to a large upstairs front room had been made before the curriculum of the future college had been decided: a pure science laboratory. Perhaps this was intended to be potentially 'one-in-the-eye' for the Russians, who were alarming us by their technological advances.
However, the college's role was to extend the teaching of science in primary school, with emphasis on Environmental Studies. So in 1964, in a sunny June, a 12 foot-long cabin stretched itself at the 'Fleetwood end' of the acres, which came with the £126,000-worth (including furniture and fittings) Lancashire County Council paid for the Home. One crossed the lawn surrounding the large greenhouse and potting-shed to attractive windowed-space for the study and teaching of geography and biology. In 1967 a further 2 acres was bought from British Rail to enable the cabins to be extended to accommodate Rural Science and a games hall. This range of sheds was extended to Derby Road giving access to a tarmacadamed car-park behind.

The Library
The largest of these sheds, its west elevation being a window looking over the fields and sky to Fleetwood, received the entire library stock in 1976. We had a man's physical strength on the library staff then, Mr Ian Sheridan. Transportation of the 35,000 volumes and runs of 270 periodicals was achieved one January day. The stock was growing by over 5000 volumes a year. It spread on the new Remploy shelving.
Now we were away from the corridor noise of the main building and there was room for all the library staff to be on show at the counter delivering the intimate service promised to the students at induction. We could see their agile figures approach from the teaching-rooms through the generous side windows.

More teaching and entertainment space: the 'New Shippon'
In 1969, building began on a major permanent extension, a free-standing brick building which later became Wyre Borough Community Centre. For the £62,000 available, the Principal and her deputy were determined to achieve maximum advantage to the college. A stage and locker-space beneath the whole was negotiated. The Queen Victoria Diamond Jubilee Arch was demolished together with the old farm shippons which students had themselves

adopted for parties and entertainments. The new building was ready for use in 1971.

This was a period when every broom-cupboard and sluice in the former adapted Home was investigated for possible teaching-space.

Application was made in 1970 for change of use of 27 Derby Road to tutorial-rooms. Local alarm that a dignified residential area might be eroded was such that a public inquiry was granted. The 5-year permit for education purposes had no need to be extended, as the house again became a family house to accommodate Mr Ralph Eaton when he was appointed Principal in 1972. He and his wife Enid organized memorable pre-lunch parties for a succession of 30 persons, where all staff could enjoy an intimate social atmosphere; it was a good settling-in.

A course to equip nursery teachers
Mr Benjamin Bee's veterinary station came on the market. The Breck Road house and various outbuildings were taken over for tutorial-rooms. The land adjoined the college front garden, so there could be access from there. One of the first courses to be taught there was launched to attract experienced infants' teachers to 'convert' to nursery education. In 1973, national policy under a Labour government, with Shirley Williams as Secretary for Education, was devised for national nursery-school provision. Miss Nancy Bowness, appointed in 1974, was in charge of this course, enthusiastically followed, for a crowded term each, by a succession of delightfully competent mature women.

The unfavourable perceived opinion (proclaimed to be erroneous by Mr Denis Healey in his autobiography *Time of my Life*) of the International Monetary Fund in 1975 had to be faced, and by 1976 the policy was thought too expensive to enact. All specialists in the study of young children do not need hindsight to form the opinion how less expensive it would have been than the social disruptions caused (in the last third of the century) by children who have had inadequate support in their early years.

In 1970, a one-year course had been established for graduates to qualify to teach in primary schools. It recruited well, building up to 60 students annually.

In 1972 two more courses were offered to experienced teachers: the Diploma of Advanced Studies in Education, under the direction of Mr Basil Butterworth, and also an in-service Bachelor of Education (BEd) course, very convenient for teachers living within the travel-area to add to their qualifications and enhance their chances of promotion.

In 1979, a workshop in the evenings was instituted under Mike Abramson to help mature students who aspired to degree-work for BA. The college library holdings were large enough, and the atmosphere and tutorial assistance within it intimate enough, to expose them to a spread of resources. The Open College had been established and courses spread through the north-west from Nelson and Colne College. Such courses were helping to make our future. Colleges of education since the mid-1970s, due to a diminishing birth-rate, were facing major changes; some were facing extinction. Poulton had been set up as a temporary college; at a time when appointments were usually permanent, it had attracted staff of flexible outlook, but there was stress and uncertainty.

In the late 1970's a Pre-Degree course of one evening study at College per week, gave confidence and an overview of resources offered for the three year B.A. Humanities Degree.
Mr. Leonard Ganley, aged 74 had already passed his first year French course with flying colours. Mr. Brian Baker (from I.C.I. Thornton) did similarly well. He stands to the right of picture with Mike Abramson, the tutor-organiser and Alec Munro who joined the B.A. course when his wife, May, finished first year studies for it.
Photo: Blackpool Evening Gazette & Herald

A happy marriage: Preston Polytechnic

After much negotiation, in 1975 the college became the Poulton Campus of the Preston Polytechnic, and many lecturing staff divided their time between Poulton, Chorley and Preston. Chorley College had merged as well, but by the end of 1976 a major decision was announced that initial teacher-training, in which so many of the staff of both colleges were involved, would be wound down (Poulton in 1980/1) and that Edge Hill College near Ormskirk would assume responsibility for in-service training. Poulton might be retained on the campus for some time by a new Humanities degree, but by 1981 education courses would finish: no more eager teachers-to-be visiting Blackpool and Fylde schools for spells of practice, and a much diminished cultural input to the growing town of Poulton. In the *Guardian* of the 25th May 1977 was written: "…Ministers are said to be genuinely surprised at the wealth and variety of

Chapter 15   Spreading

innovation they are poised to destroy..." From the 1960s, educationalists had come from the United States to see what was achieved in our primary schools, where a curriculum was advised rather than imposed. In the USA, corporate man could move from state to state with his family finding the same text-books for the same grades. Our British fluidity allowed innovation, originality and regional variation, even another language - as in Wales.

When Ralph Eaton succeeded Miss Mary Wilson as Principal in 1972, selected from open competition by very democratic interviewing procedures, no-one then knew that one of his tasks would be the winding-down of the college, as he became Assistant Director at Preston Polytechnic, and the centralisation of courses there.

Ralph Eaton
During his retirement at Milnthorpe

Some staff must depart. They were assisted by the Principal's detached circumspection and his scrutinizing lawyer-like attitude. An enforced leaving of a community which absorbed so much of one's talents and personality is a type of bereavement, but with this sympathetic counsellor and friend, no-one was utterly discouraged.

He must have written dozens of references, undeterred from composing a different and relevant one for each job application before an appropriate slot was achieved. The individual counselling in the pleasant office in the 18th century portion of the college building, where Matron Bury had presided, was never hurried, before he walked in the evening to the Principal's accommodation in Derby Road. So conscientious was he, that he was concerned for those who made their own arrangements without his listening ear. Such a one was the late Miss Dorothy Smith, who moved her home to Cockersands then soon came back to Poulton town to be as busy as ever in the music scene.

B.A. Humanities Degree
Meanwhile, there was much to do at Poulton Campus. As soon as the BA Humanities was approved for English in 1978, rapid additions to the library were made incorporating stock from Chorley College. All the teaching of English and a good proportion of Linguistics was conducted at Poulton concurrently with BEd (which finished at Poulton in 1980/1).
New staff and library resources came to support subjects offered in the BA degree, which had not been taught at Poulton before. The Political Science department at Preston, headed by Alastair Thomas, brought the subject to Poulton in 1979. One of the staff, Terry Hopton, came to Poulton full-time and was soon integrated into the social life. Seven tutors brought their own specialisms, including Economics. The Polytechnic welcomed this diversification in the School of Economics & Business Studies as leading to increased expansion in these subjects in the institution.
Education Studies in the BA was a very popular choice of mature students, its methodology being common to other subjects such as Linguistics, and combining well with Politics, Economics and History. Tutors who had taught Psychology and Sociology of Education, and Philosophy for the BEd glided easily into the BA role.

Knowing as we do now that the BA Humanities flourished and formed the basis for a much larger modular degree, it is difficult to recall the uncertainties. Our David Foster, Head of the History department, was told by the late Dr Law, Director of the Polytechnic, that he was making in 1979 a wise move to Hull College of Higher Education to be Head of Humanities there. Going through 'more name-changes than a much married film-star' the institution became the University of Lincoln. David's career and varied experience developed with it. He finally became International Quality Manager and still does (in retirement) moderation work for the University's overseas programmes. He writes that his memories of Poulton College "…are legion. One of the main things …was the developing interest in local and regional history, especially the introduction of fieldwork into the History programme and the incorporation of History into the Environmental Studies alternative course. I recall field trips to Hadrian's Wall, the Cotswolds and Gloucester, York (twice), Durham, Shropshire and the Norfolk Broads with great affection. It was on such occasions that one really came to know the students." The department's work in the Fylde led to his booklet *Excursions into Fylde History* (Hendon Press, Nelson 1976). "I was also fortunate in receiving much encouragement for my own research including a sabbatical term, and I have Poulton College to thank for providing the environment in which to obtain my doctorate.... I also learned a great deal from Peter Long. The Local History Teachers' Group that he founded c1969 I was able to continue after he left. That also provided a number of excellent contacts with local secondary schools."

History

The BA degree in History recruited well. One of the 1978 intake was awarded a first class degree. There was tragic loss with the death of Tim Curtis, appointed Head & Course Leader in David Foster's place, but Mike Abramson, Anne Brownlow, Christine King, Rex Pope, Jeff Timmins and Jack Watson gave long service.

Mr. Jack Watson joined Poulton history staff in 1968. Interested in world affairs generally, his text books are particularly helpful to students of the history of modern times.
See bibliography.
Photo: Herald Weekly May 1974

Four of Poulton's staff joined the Division of Foreign Language and Literature at Preston. Responsibility for consultation with students of French for the BA on Poulton Campus was with Peter Edwards. He, with the late Barrie Preston, Robert Davies and Alan Godfrey, gave long and enthusiastic service. They assisted with the Diploma course for Bilingual Secretaries.

Also Poulton could offer a well-equipped library. During the early days when courses were moderated at Manchester University, Robert Davies had diligently frequented university bookshops and selected modern publications in literature, particularly the French novel so that our holdings were very relevant and attractive for contemporary studies.

Geography and Combined Sciences

The subject of geography, when the BEd was being phased out, was finding a future not only in the BA Humanities but also in the BSc Combined Sciences (from 1983). The Planning and Built Environment Certificate were also supported. Staff replacements were made with this in mind, so the tutorial staff - six in all with two full-time technical assistants and a cartographer appointed from 1981 - had continuity of working on the Poulton Campus until the move to Preston in summer 1983: Howard Phillips, Brian Bristow, Rob Webster, David Longworth, Mike Clark and Mike Pearson (who was appointed to the Polytechnic in 1975).

Foreign Language and Literature
see chapter 7

English

In 1981, in adjudicating aptitude for the BA course, Andor Gomme, Reader in English in the University of Keele, found most students to be fully up to degree work, and that two were working at or near honours degree level. His predictions were justified.

This subject, underpinning all work in school, had been given an enthusiastic start in 1963 by the late E. L. Black. He was later appointed as Principal of a Durham college. His own captivating prose on such a topic as Roman roads which he liked to explore, could occasionally be seen in the Guardian newspaper.

As late as 2003, some former Poulton students will recognise the names of Daniel Lamont who became acting Dean in the Faculty of Cultural, Legal and Social Studies within the Humanities Department at UCLan, and Brian Rosebury and Jane Darcy (Jane is now a specialist in British Children's Literature) who came as bright young things in the 1970s to Poulton. They work within a team of people who offer such a list of wide-ranging modules in English literature - which needs a down-load from the internet to discover.

How much of this development is due to the teacher-training enthusiasm during the past 40 years from the spread of love of stories and poetry in the first schools?

Chapter 15   Spreading

In 1972 Miss Mary Wilson retired from her post as Principal. She donated a bed of azaleas, in the background is the "new shippon" and the house where she lived, the latter used generously for visitor accommodation, entertainment and for important meetings.

Bibliography

CARPENTER, Humphrey The envy of the world. Fifty years of the BBC Third Programme and Radio 4.

FOSTER, David Excursions into Fylde history Hendon Press, Nelson (1976)

HEALEY, Denis The time of my life (1989) 07181 311 4 2

HEARNDEN, Arthur ed. The British in Germany, educational reconstruction after 1945 Hamish Hamilton (1978) 0241 89637 1

JENKINS, Roy Life at the centre (1991) 0333 551 64 8

JOYCE, Patrick Visions of the people. Industrial England and the question of class 1840-1914 0521 371 52 C.U.P.

LANCASHIRE EVENING POST 24th July 1972 A life of dedication (A feature on Miss M H Wilson on the occasion of her retirement)

POPE, Rex and PHILLIPS, Ken University of Central Lancashire: a history of the development of the Institution since 1828 (1995) Preston: University of Central Lancashire

PRESTON-DUNLOP, Valerie Rudolph Laban. An extraordinary life Dance Books (1998) 1 85273 060 9

STOREY, Christine Poulton-le-Fylde Tempus Publishing (2001)

STOREY, Christine Poulton Church heritage, the church of Poulton, Carleton and Hardhorn Poulton-le-Fylde History Society (1988)

WALTON, John K Blackpool (1998) Edinburgh University Press

WALTON, J K The Blackpool landlady: a social history Manchester (1978)

WATSON, Jack B Success in British history since 1914 John Murray (1983) 0 7196 3924 2

WATSON, Jack B The West Indian heritage John Murray (1979)

WISEMAN, David Poulton-le-Fylde once upon a time (1979)

WILSON, Mary Hamilton 1912-2001 After the War was over: Memories of the British Control Commission in Germany. The author (1952) Typescript autobiography, 2nd floor archives at University of Central Lancashire 943.0894

Index

Abbott, Kenneth	74, 82	Borland, Mr. Archie & Mrs. Ann	40
Abramson, Mike	97		
Accrington	16	Bowness, Nancy	96
Alegaard, Buffie	89	Boyle, Sir Edward	44
Amalgamated Weavers Association	3,5,7,16	Bradbury, Ray	86
		Breck Farm House	3, 5, 22
Alexandra, Princess	92	Breckan Magazine	55
Allied Control Commission	40	Breyman, Dr. Oker Institute, Germany	42
Amery, Rt. Hon. Julian	50	Brigsbury, Mrs	30
Antwerp	40	Bristow, Brian	101
Astin, Enid	36,67,90	British Aerospace	57
Australia	61	Brooks, Denis	63, ff.
Baker, Brian	58,97	Brownlow, Anne	100
Bamber Bridge	58	Buick	36
Barnes, Brian	73	Burrell, Doreen (Alcock)	72
Battye, Gerald	67		
Beatles	62, 56	Bury, James, & Dorcas Ellen	16,17,28, 32, ff.
Bennett Valerie (Mrs. Bateson)	21,26,78		
		Butterworth, Basil	96
Berlin	43	Byrom, Messrs. James Ltd.	9
Berry, Scott	55		
Bee, Benjamin	96	Carey Arthur Cyril	18,34,36
Betjeman, John	31	Carroll, Lewis	49
Bilsborough Hall	91	Caton	34
Black, E.L.	101	Cheetham, Mrs. Sybil	71
Blackburn Cemetery	7	Chorley College	58,97,99
Blackburn & District Weavers Association	5	Christmas	35,36,80
		Clark, Mike	101
Blackburn Library	6	Clayton – le – Woods	28
Blackburn Weekly Telegraph	5	Clitheroe	7
		Clough, Fred	73
Blackpool Gazette & Herald	9	Colne	89
		Commonwealth visitors	92
Blackpool landlady	52	Connaughton, Agnes	71
Bolton, Len	67	Conservative Association, Blackpool	87
Bond, Miss Elsie	26, 66		
Booth, James	52, 71	Cooperative Society	25,32

Cotton Industries Board	30	Gibson. Bert	29,37
Cotton Industries Convalescent Home	20	Gill, Arthur	67
		Glasgow University	41
Coward, Noel	90	Glastonbury	68
Cross, Joseph	5,6,7,8,24	Goddard, Tony	90
Curtis, Peter	69	Godfrey, Alan	58,100
Curtis, Tim	100	Greenwood, Paul	52
Darcy, Jane	101	Gomme Andor	101
Darwen, Victor	21,25,29,81	Hadfield, Victor	ii
Davies, Robert	54,55,100	Hall, Dr. F	16,19,35
De Gaulle, Charles	54,93	Halliwell estate	5,15
Derby, Lord	92	Harley, Kay	90
Derby Road	30	Harris Museum, Preston	73
Doughty, Philip	73	Harrison, Ray	80
Dublin	83	Haworth, W. Yorks.	90
Dutch	35,91	Healey, Denis	96
Eaton, Ralph	2,46,96,98	Heaton, Robert	i,17
Economics	99	Holt Jackson, Lytham	84
Edge Hill College	97	Henderson, A. MP	7
Edwards, Peter	58,100	Hill, David	61
Elk at Highfurlong	73	Hiroshima	47
Ellis, Lilian	52	Holmes, Christine	60
Ellison, George	72	Hooley, Thomas	1,15,27,32-37, 51,69,92
Environmental Studies	73,95,99,100		
European Economic Community	54	Howard & Bullogh	6
		Hopton, Terry	99
Evans, Charles T.	74	Hungary	91
Ewan, John	69	Hunt, Noreen	26,78
Farnworth, Warren	61,83	I.C.I. Thornton	97
Foster, David	71,99,100	Jackson, Ronald	86,93
French Courses	58	Japan	91
Fylde Academy of Young Musicians	63	Judges Lodgings Museum, Lancaster	87
Ganley, Leonard	58,97	Keele University	29,39,40-42
Gardner, Arthur	74	Kelly, Pat	91
Gardner, Mrs. May	25,26,78	Kendal Milne Family	51
Gartside, Mrs. Jeremy	52	Kilmarnock	39,41
General Strike	7	King, Christine	100
Germany	41-43	Kirkham	50,74
Gibbs Bookshop, Manchester	84	Knott End	52

Lamont, Daniel	101	Nawaliska, Mrs. Sybil	71
Lancashire County Council	11,33,78, 79,82	Formerly Mrs. Cheetham	
		Nelson & Colne College	97
Lancashire Library	84	Niagara Falls	90
Lancaster University	54,69,70,91	Normandy	34
Lancastria School of Management	91	Oddfellows	8
		Oldham, David	56
Law, Dr. Harry	70,99	Open College	97
Lawrenson, Ronja, Dutch visitor	42	Open University	50,88
		Ordinance Survey	12,13
Lee, Jennie	50	O'Shea, Tessie	30
Leith	41	Panzer, Dr. Frau	13
Life Long Learning	50	Paris	55,56
Linguistics	99	Parry, Henry Isaacson	4
Local Studies	86, 99	Parry, Judge	5
Lodgings	78,79	Peacock, Peter	61
Long, Peter	21,26,67, 83,87	Pearson, Mike	101
		Penin, Bernard	59
Longworth, David	101	Phillips, Howard	101
Lord, Sir Percy	21	Picken, Mollie	61
Lytham St. Annes	62	Pilling C of E Junior School	72
Macmillon, Harold PM	21,50	Plug	91
Malham	76	Political Science	99
Mallett, Gillian	59,72,88	Pope, Rex	100
Manchester University	54	Post-Graduate Certificate	58
Manifold, Margery	66	Mr. Potts, Poulton Architect	87
Mary Macarthur Home	27	Preston Polytechnic	63
Masonic Lodge, Poulton	17	Preston Institute for the Diffusion of Knowledge (1828)	92
Mayhew, Tom	73		
Midland, Michigan	90		
Miners	7,19	Preston, Barry	58,100
Monaghan, Mary-Alice	88	R.A.F.	34,35
Morecambe	1,4,20,24,29	Railway	4,8,48,95
Morgue	35	Reed's grocers	51
Morris, William	9	Rhoden, John	58
Moulins, France	57	Revoe Primary School: chess	72
Munro, Alec and May	97	Richard's Hardware	51
Murray, Dr. A.R.	16	Rolfe, Gifford	61
Myers, Mr. And Mrs.	20,27	Roper, Geoffrey	73
Naesmith, Sir Andrew	16,32	Roseacre Junior School	72

Rosebury, Brian	101	University of Central Lancs, Preston	40
Rubella	34	Usher, Nora	26,71
Rural Science	86,95	USSR: visitors	91
Saginaw Valley State College, Michigan	89	Utrecht	91
Sanderson, Chris	80	Uttley, Jack	33
St. Chad's Poulton	35,63,69	Victoria Hospital, Blackpool	35,49
Scobie, Miss	30,82	War Memorial Fund, Cotton Industry	20
Scholey, Mr. Tony	73	Ward, Joe	37,60
Shackleton, Sir David J. MP	7	Watkins, Sue	56
Sheridan, Ian	ii,95	Watson, Jack	100
Singleton Lodge	79	Webster, Rob	101
Skipool Creek	4	Welch, Paul	94
Smith, Dorothy	64,99	Whitehead, Rev. Derek	63,67
Sorbonne, The	56	Whittaker, Prof. W.L.	89
Sorn, Ayreshire	40	Whittle-le-Woods	29
South Africa: Dr. Naguran	91	Wignall, Dr. Margaret	49
Southport	9	Wilkinson, Betty	71
Stepney, East. St. George's School	43	Williams, Shirley	96
Stephenson, Mrs. Brenda	26,78	Wilson, Mary Hamilton	3,24,39-47
Stone, Brian	56,60	Windermere	74,75
Suffolk, Mrs. Winifred	78	Woodlands	4,8
Tandberg Language laboratory	55	Worsley, Christine	ii,88
Thatcher, Margaret	50	Wycoller	89
Thomas, Alastair	99	Wyre Borough Community Centre	95
Thompson, Mr. (Pleasure Beach)	86,92	Wyre Borough	i
Thorney, J.B. architect	8,9,10,11	Wiseman, Prof. Stephen	21
Thornton I.C.I. plant	59		
Timmins, Jeff	100		
Tito (Trieste)	47		
Tomlins, Gill	62		
Tomlinson, Ellis	87		
Toronto	90		
Trade Unions	5,48		
Trades' Council, Blackpool	33		
Trueman, Bryan	61		
Tyler, Arthur	33		